Europe's Place in Global Financial Governance after the Crisis

In the years leading up to the global financial crisis, the European Union (EU) had emerged as a central actor in global financial governance, almost rivalling the United States in influence. While the USA and the EU continue to dominate financial rule setting in the post-crisis world, the context in which they do so has changed dramatically. Pre-crisis ideas about laissez-faire regulation have been discredited in favour of more interventionist ones. The G20 and the Financial Stability Board have been charged with stronger coordination of global efforts. At the same time, jurisdictions have re-emphasized the need 'to get their own regulatory house in order' before committing to further global harmonization. And through bank failures and massive bail-outs, the financial sector – hitherto a driving force behind the cross-border integration of finance – has been reconfigured.

This book asks a straightforward question: what have these and other key post-crisis trends in global finance done to the position that the European Union occupies in it? The contributions to this book analyse the link between financial governance in the European Union and on the global level from diverse theoretical angles, and they cover the main issues that will shape the future European role on the global regulatory stage.

This book was originally published as a special issue of the *Journal of European Public Policy*.

Daniel Mügge is an Associate Professor at the Political Science Department of the University of Amsterdam and a Researcher at the Amsterdam Institute for Social Science Research.

Journal of European Public Policy Series
Series Editor: Jeremy Richardson is a Professor at Nuffield College, Oxford University

This series seeks to bring together some of the finest edited works on European Public Policy. Reprinting from Special Issues of the *Journal of European Public Policy*, the focus is on using a wide range of social sciences approaches, both qualitative and quantitative, to gain a comprehensive and definitive understanding of Public Policy in Europe.

Towards a Federal Europe
Edited by Alexander H. Trechsel

The Disparity of European Integration
Edited by Tanja A. Börzel

Cross-National Policy Convergence
Causes Concepts and Empirical Findings
Edited by Christoph Knill

Civilian or Military Power?
European Foreign Policy in Perspective
Edited by Helene Sjursen

The European Union and New Trade Politics
Edited by John Peterson and Alasdair R. Young

Comparative Studies of Policy Agendas
Edited by Frank R. Baumgartner, Christoffer Green-Pedersen and Bryan D. Jones

The Constitutionalization of the European Union
Edited by Berthold Rittberger and Frank Schimmelfenig

Empirical and Theoretical Studies in EU Lobbying
Edited by David Coen

Mutual Recognition as a New Mode of Governance
Edited by Susanne K. Schmidt

France and the European Union
Edited by Emiliano Grossman

Immigration and Integration Policy in Europe
Edited by Tim Bale

Reforming the European Commission
Edited by Michael W. Bauer

International Influence Beyond Conditionality
Postcommunist Europe after EU enlargement
Edited by Rachel A. Epstein and Ulrich Sedelmeier

The Role of Political Parties in the European Union
Edited by Björn Lindberg, Anne Rasmussen and Andreas Warntjen

EU External Governance
Projecting EU Rules beyond Membership
Edited by Sandra Lavenex and Frank Schimmelfennig

EMU and Political Science
What Have We Learned?
Edited by Henrik Enderlein and Amy Verdun

Learning and Governance in the EU Policy Making Process
Edited by Anthony R. Zito

Political Representation and EU Governance
Edited by Peter Mair and Jacques Thomassen

Europe and the Management of Globalization
Edited by Wade Jacoby and Sophie Meunier

Negotiation Theory and the EU
The State of the Art
Edited by Andreas Dür, Gemma Mateo and Daniel C. Thomas

The Political Economy of Europe's Incomplete Single Market
Edited by David Howarth and Tal Sadeh

The European Union's Foreign Economic Policies
A Principal-Agent Perspective
Edited by Andreas Dür and Michael Elsig

The Politics of the Lisbon Agenda Governance
Architectures and Domestic Usages of Europe
Edited by Susana Borrás and Claudio M. Radaelli

Agency Governance in the European Union
Edited by Berthold Rittberger and Arndt Wonka

The EU Timescape
Edited by Klaus H. Goetz and Jan-Hinrik Meyer-Sahling

The EU's Common Foreign and Security Policy
Edited by Helene Sjursen

Economic Patriotism in Open Economies
Edited by Ben Clift and Cornelia Woll

The Power of the European Court of Justice
Edited by Susanne K. Schmidt and R. Daniel Kelemen

The Representative Turn in EU Studies
Edited by Sandra Kröger and Dawid Friedrich

Legislative Co-decision in the European Union
Edited by Anne Rasmussen, Charlotte Burns and Christine Reh

Frameworks of the European Union's Policy Process
Edited by Nikolaos Zahariadis

Changing Models of Capitalism in Europe and the US
Edited by Richard Deeg and Gregory Jackson

Europe's Place in Global Financial Governance after the Crisis
Edited by Daniel Mügge

The European Union: Integration and Enlargement
Edited by R. Daniel Kelemen, Anand Menon and Jonathan Slapin

Europe's Place in Global Financial Governance after the Crisis

Edited by
Daniel Mügge

Routledge
Taylor & Francis Group
LONDON AND NEW YORK

First published 2015 by Routledge

2 Park Square, Milton Park, Abingdon, Oxon, OX14 4RN
605 Third Avenue, New York, NY 10017

Routledge is an imprint of the Taylor & Francis Group, an informa business

First issued in paperback 2020

British Library Cataloguing in Publication Data
A catalogue record for this book is available from the British Library

ISBN 13: 978-1-138-80349-7 (hbk)
ISBN 13: 978-0-367-73936-2 (pbk)

Typeset in Sabon
by RefineCatch Limited, Bungay, Suffolk

Publisher's Note
The publisher accepts responsibility for any inconsistencies that may have arisen during the conversion of this book from journal articles to book chapters, namely the possible inclusion of journal terminology.

Contents

Citation Information

The chapters in this book were originally published in the *Journal of European Public Policy*, volume 21, issue 3 (March 2014). When citing this material, please use the original page numbering for each article, as follows:

Chapter 1
Europe's regulatory role in post-crisis global finance
Daniel Mügge
Journal of European Public Policy, volume 21, issue 3 (March 2014) pp. 316–326

Chapter 2
The sources of European Union influence in international financial regulatory fora
Lucia Quaglia
Journal of European Public Policy, volume 21, issue 3 (March 2014) pp. 327–345

Chapter 3
Shattered expectations: the defeat of European ambitions of global financial reform
Hans-Jürgen Bieling
Journal of European Public Policy, volume 21, issue 3 (March 2014) pp. 346–366

Chapter 4
Losing abroad but winning at home: European financial industry groups in global financial governance since the crisis
Kevin Young
Journal of European Public Policy, volume 21, issue 3 (March 2014) pp. 367–388

Chapter 5
Distinctions, affiliations, and professional knowledge in financial reform expert groups
Leonard Seabrooke and Eleni Tsingou
Journal of European Public Policy, volume 21, issue 3 (March 2014) pp. 389–407

Chapter 6
Experimentalism in European Union and global financial governance: interactions, contrasts, and implications
Malcolm Campbell-Verduyn and Tony Porter
Journal of European Public Policy, volume 21, issue 3 (March 2014) pp. 408–429

Chapter 7
The European Union as hardening agent: soft law and the diffusion of global financial regulation
Abraham Newman and David Bach
Journal of European Public Policy, volume 21, issue 3 (March 2014) pp. 430–452

Please direct any queries you may have about the citations to clsuk.permissions@cengage.com

Europe's regulatory role in post-crisis global finance

Daniel Mügge

ABSTRACT Before the crisis, the European Union (EU) had emerged as a major force in global financial governance (GFG). The contributions to this collection examine the different dimensions of the EU's role in GFG and how they have been affected by the recent crisis. Taking a bird's eye view, this introduction offers three main arguments. First, the EU has stabilized, rather than challenged, established ideas in and approaches to GFG. Second, the EU continues to be one of two central nodes in GFG, which essentially still is a transatlantic affair – confounding expectations that Europe would find itself in a much more dispersed web of links with other regulatory powers around the world. Third, given its special institutional character, there are signs that a prominent EU may transform the *modus operandi* of GFG itself, but given present centrifugal forces it remains unclear how pronounced these dynamics will be.

INTRODUCTION

Seven years after the financial crisis erupted in the 2007, global financial governance (GFG) has entered calmer waters. Work on regulatory challenges such as shadow banking continues. But the enormous uncertainty surrounding the direction of future reforms and heated debates it inspired have made way for a translation of regulatory contours, agreed in the Group of 20 (G20) and other institutions, into concrete policy.

From a European perspective, the challenge to global financial governance that the crisis has posed arrived at an interesting moment: on the one hand, the European Union (EU) had acquired increasing clout on the global stage. On the other hand, the crisis was widely seen as one of 'the West', including Europe, that accelerated a shift of power from OECD countries to the BRICS-countries – Brazil, Russia, India, China and South Africa – in particular. So is the EU's star in GFG rising or declining? And how well does such a power-centred perspective capture Europe's role in GFG in the first place, given that its institutional architecture makes it an international actor unlike any other?

The contributions to this collection tackle these questions by examining the contours of Europe's place in global financial governance as it takes shape in these immediate post-crisis years. They cover a broad spectrum both theoretically and methodologically. Quaglia shows how the EU's influence in GFG has depended on the coherence of the member states' preferences. Bieling shifts the focus to these preferences themselves and analyses why a stronger reform impetus, which many observers had expected from the EU after the crisis, has not materialized. Young zooms in on one aspect of politics that is often seen as particularly relevant to such preference formation: using innovative scholarly tools, he maps the influence of the European financial sector in affecting policy outcomes. Also Seabrooke and Tsingou study Europe in a global context, but instead of firms they study ideas. They show how the debate about the origins and necessary responses to the crisis has been a truly transnational one, in which favoured explanations and solutions defy clear geographical mapping in line with putatively more or less statist traditions in countries on either side of the Atlantic. The final two contributions focus on the impact of Europe, as an institutionally unique actor, on GFG. Campbell-Verduyn and Porter explore the degree to which experimentalist governance, increasingly established in Europe, might travel to regulatory politics at the global level. And Newman and Bach reverse the perspective, showing how the EU can 'harden' international soft law agreements when it translates them into binding rules for its member states.

This introduction draws on the insights of these contributions, as well as those of other scholarship, to offer an encompassing assessment of how, in a post-crisis environment, the European Union as a pole in global financial regulation relates to the rest of the world. As it argues, a broad range of factors have led the EU to stabilize, rather than challenge, established ideas in and approaches to GFG. The EU also continues to be one of two central nodes in GFG, which essentially still is a transatlantic affair – confounding expectations that Europe would find itself in a much more dispersed web of links with other regulatory powers around the world. Finally, given its special institutional character, the EU may find itself transforming the *modus operandi* of GFG itself, but given centrifugal forces it remains unclear how pronounced these dynamics will be.

EUROPE AS AN INTELLECTUAL STABILIZER IN GFG

The global financial crisis constitutes a watershed in our thinking about the global political economy, comparable to the years 1979/1980, when Ronald Reagan and Margret Thatcher assumed leadership in the United States of America (USA) and the United Kingdom (UK) and ushered in what many think of as a neoliberal era. It was a crisis in the literal sense that real uncertainty prevailed about what the future would hold – whether the prevailing economic order would survive or be replaced by something else.

When the crisis was most acute – in late 2008 and 2009 – it fed speculation among some observers about a complete overhaul of financial rules and governance; others expected business as usual amid minimal reforms. The actual result falls somewhere in between (Moschella and Tsingou 2013). As it turned out, policy-makers on both sides of the Atlantic have tried to stabilize domestic financial systems without fundamentally altering the way in which they relate to the rest of the economy and society (*cf.* Mügge forthcoming). As of 2014 we know that, relative to the depth of the crisis, rather little has changed in global financial affairs. That becomes clear once we consider the forces that might have disrupted global financial governance much more seriously than has actually happened.

First, the crisis has widely been interpreted as a failure of a free-market paradigm that had been espoused and promoted by the United States and later also the European Union. Financial deregulation was seen as an important culprit of the crisis. On that basis, it would have been plausible that the USA, as the most important and consequential champion of financial deregulation, would have lost legitimacy and authority in global financial governance. Europe might have concluded that 'the American way of financial governance' had been tried and had failed – and that the reconstruction of the European financial system would call for a fundamentally different approach (*cf.* Bieling 2014).

In addition, not only in the USA and the UK but also on the European Continent, financial deregulation had been linked to widening inequality, both as a source (Hacker and Pierson 2010; Rajan 2010) and as an indirect consequence (Crouch 2009; Young 2009) – trying to camouflage inequality by easy access to credit for the less well-off. And an out of kilter financial system had been blamed on systematic underinvestment in productive resources, contributing to the long-term decline of the productive base and hence a dangerous reliance on financial services as a source (highly concentrated) corporate profits. Observers who had seen the crisis as an opportunity to transform Western economies more fundamentally could not but be disappointed by the actual reforms – even if the more misanthropic among them were not altogether surprised.

This belief that Europe somehow stood for a 'different' approach to financial regulation, and that it would pursue that, potentially without extensive transatlantic co-ordination, had been fed by the (exaggerated) notion that Continental Europe's economies were, at heart, fundamentally different than 'Anglo-American' ones. Institutionalist comparative political economy literature (most prominently Hall and Soskice [2001]) had often been understood as suggesting that Germany and France had an economic DNA, as it were, that had always been difficult to square with financial deregulation, and that would let the EU as a whole gravitate back towards a re-embedding of financial markets.

Historically, financial regulation has indeed been closely linked to other dimensions of national economic governance, for example industrial policy (Zysman 1983). In the course of financial regulatory reform since the early 1990s, such positive co-ordination (Jayasuriya 2001) has played a smaller role, however, than institutionalist thinking might have suggested (Mügge 2010). Even if Germany, for example, can in important respects be described as a co-ordinated market economy, its regulatory preferences have not been dictated by regulation's interaction with some 'German model of capitalism' at large. Instead, such preferences are often best understood as a combination of the preferences of domestic firms (Mügge and Stellinga [2010]; critically Young [2012]) and specific, rather than general, effects that reforms would have in a country, for example on its pension system or the real estate market. Given the diversity of economic and institutional structures among EU member states, the latter frequently were at odds about the 'European course' in GFG, weakening the European voice on the global stage (see Quaglia 2014).

In consequence, Europe did not emerge as an important source of 'alternative thinking' about global financial regulation. As Seabrooke and Tsingou (2014) document in this collection, the various reports about the shortcomings of global financial governance and remedies that appeared at the height of the crisis do not follow a putative market-friendly versus market-sceptical divide that could be mapped onto more versus less interventionist governments in Europe and beyond. At the paradigmatic level Europe has not emerged as an alternative pole that would propagate a different line than the USA or the EU itself had done prior to the crisis.

In addition, because stabilizing financial systems has been the main impetus of policy, rather than simply getting financial regulation 'right', regulatory tools have been used alongside unorthodox monetary policy. For that reason, the effectiveness of reforms has become difficult to judge. Negative real interest rates have put asset markets, banks and whole economies on life support, and there is no agreement about how long such support can last and what happens once it is withdrawn. In policy terms, ultra-loose monetary policy has entered *terra incognita*. It seems nigh impossible to establish what kinds of regulations are really necessary for a stable financial system while the value of banks' assets is underwritten by a gigantic monetary stimulus programme. The net effect has been to take pressure off policy-makers to subject a figuratively and literally bankrupt financial system to more branch and roots reform. Loose monetary policy has made a modest reform package look viable that may still turn out not to be so.

Concerning Europe's role in global financial governance, both of these dynamics have had a similar effect: the relatively modest reform ambition has obviated the perceived need for a very tight co-ordination of policy with most other major forces in GFG. And as governments and central banks have underwritten their own financial firms, they have integrated financial regulation and supervision with other forms of economic policy, for example concerning pension reforms or housing policies. Even though we will not return to the pre-liberalization days of positive co-ordination of economic policies (Jayasuriya 2001), there is a lot more co-ordination between regulation and other forms of financial market policy now than there was just before the crisis. The ensuing 're-embedding' of regulation mitigates against formal global agreements that do not leave space for such embedding.

Ironically, then, it was the depth of the crisis that made reforms unacceptable that would have compromised short-term financial stability. To borrow a medial metaphor, open-heart surgery on the European financial system was not a viable option when the patient – the European economy and the European project (think of uncertain future UK membership) – was in critical condition. As a result, the EU as a whole emerged as a stabilizing force in global regulatory debates more than as an innovator (Mügge 2013).

BIPOLAR GLOBAL FINANCIAL GOVERNANCE

The continued EU–US agreement on many basic parameters of financial governance matters especially because – against the expectations of many – global financial governance has essentially remained a transatlantic affair even though, after the fall of Lehman Brothers in 2008, the G20 had been assigned the guiding role in the global reform efforts.

In the wake of the so-called Asian financial crisis the much more circumscribed Group of 7 (G7) had established the Financial Stability Forum (FSF) in 1999, which later was transformed into the Financial Stability Board (FSB). After that crisis, reform efforts concentrated on agreeing on a set of standards and codes (eventually compiled in the FSF Compendium) that should improve domestic financial governance in South-East Asia in particular. For many countries in the region, however, the imposition of reforms in combination with other IMF-mandated structural reform programmes delegitimized global financial governance (*cf.* Underhill and Zhang 2003). By the time the credit crisis hit North American and Europe, many countries outside 'the West' had developed a cynical view on GFG, viewing it as skewed and exclusive.

At least on the face of it, the growing prominence of the G20 was a gesture by the G7 countries to open up international deliberations to a range of countries from around the world. It is ironic that many emerging market economies were invited to the table when the most important agenda item – the crisis response – concerned them much less than the US and the EU. The main expectation was that global financial governance would finally live up to its name by including clearly audible voices and perspectives from BRICS countries, if not second-tier emerging markets like Indonesia and Argentina.

Such a shift from transatlantic to truly global financial governance has not taken place. Certainly considering financial regulation, as the contributions to this collection do, standard-setting in, for example, the Basel Committee continues to be dominated by the USA and Europe. The same is true for other policy fields, for example derivatives regulation or accounting standards. The expectation that the EU would become one of maybe half a dozen nodes in a multilateral GFG regime has turned out wrong.

Several factors account for this pattern: most obviously, the North Atlantic region has been hardest hit by the crisis. The countries in that region host the world's most important market places for wholesale finance. They are home to finance-relevant sectors such as global accounting firms and credit rating agencies. The countries in the region have also been among the most financialized, such that financial re-regulation or otherwise has had more profound implications for their future economic trajectories – think, for example, of private-debt-fuelled real estate markets as a past motor of growth.

Equally important is the deep interpenetration of European and American financial markets. American investment banks are prominent players in European markets. The reverse is also true, even if the number of European firms in the Wall Street top tier is a lot smaller. Securities exchanges have merged or co-operate across the Atlantic. Both from the perspective of smooth transactions between firms as well as business operations within them, a seamless transatlantic integration of financial markets is imperative (cf. Young 2014). The high degree of transatlantic market integration implies the need for careful fine-tuning of the interaction between rules – much more so than along any other inter-regional regulatory axis.

The low prominence of China in global financial governance, and regulatory matters in particular, should be seen in this light. Chinese banks have quickly become more visible in global finance over the recent years. But there are no signs that they will be released from the specific role that they have in the Chinese development model and encouraged or even allowed to operate as purely profit-oriented enterprises. To the degree that global regulatory policy co-ordination is animated by concerns about the international competitiveness of domestic firms (Singer 2007), the low profile China keeps in global financial regulation is not particularly puzzling.

At the same time, the comparison with the German and French historical experiences may be instructive for future developments in this realm. Both countries became prominent voices in regional and global regulatory debates when their large banks were disembedded from relatively tight domestic policy co-ordination and became 'market players' first and foremost. An intense Chinese involvement in global regulatory politics is thus to be expected only once regulatory mismatches, instead of overt and direct government intervention, become the most relevant determinant for cross-border market access for Chinese firms abroad and foreign banks in China. *Mutatis mutandis*, this line of argument applies to other prominent emerging market economies. For the foreseeable future, then, the EU is thus likely to remain one of two poles in global financial regulation.

THE EUROPEAN INFLUENCE ON GLOBAL FINANCIAL GOVERNANCE BEYOND POWER POLITICS

While both intellectually and in terms of main actors there is remarkable continuity between the pre-crisis and post-crisis periods, the proclaimed aims and *modus operandi* of GFG have changed repeatedly over the past decades – affecting also GFG's relevance for the EU and the EU's position in it.

Once the FSF had compiled its Compendium, the urgency of more intense global co-operation waned around 2002. The years between 1999 and 2002 had stood in the sign of technocratic global rule harmonization in the name of implementing best practice. Soon thereafter, however, complacency set in

(Helleiner and Pagliari 2010). While paying lip-service to best practice, its implementation on the ground often fell short (Mosley 2010; Walter 2010). Flagship harmonization initiatives, such as the one between the International Accounting Standards Board and its American counterpart, the US Financial Accounting Standards Board, lost steam. The crisis since 2007 has rekindled the interest in global harmonization, now conceived not so much as a sharing of best practice, but as a concerted effort to confront what has since then been seen as a collective action problem. The G20 has spearheaded this effort. Before long, however, the dominant mode of regulatory reform shifted from maximum rule harmonization to mutual adaptation and recognition based on minimum standards (Helleiner and Pagliari 2011). This shift from harmonization to mutual adaptation has followed both from the heavy government involvement in the financial sector during the crisis (bank bail-outs in particular) and from the recognition that regulating with an eye to (systemic) financial stability requires a modicum of flexibility on behalf of supervisory and regulatory authorities. A one-size-fits-all regulatory straightjacket is no longer seen as appropriate (The Warwick Commission on International Financial Reform 2009).

Given these shifts, the choice the EU confronts is no longer one between harmonization and potentially detrimental regulatory competition. Instead, the challenge is to eradicate discontinuities between domestic policy regimes that might otherwise undermine regulatory policy goals. At the same time, the EU has to give domestic authorities sufficient space to attune policy to domestic circumstances, both structural ones and those relating, for example, to the business cycle.

For the EU, this challenge is not new. Opinions differ about how successfully it has combined policy coherence with sensitivity for member-state-level diversity in the past. But the EU undeniably has developed tools to address this tension. Many directives, for example, leave room for national authorities to fine-tune implementation measures. The 2000 Lisbon Summit endorsed the Open Method of Co-ordination (OMC); since then, instruments like peer review and revisable benchmarks have grown in popularity. More generally, scholars have argued for an ascendance of 'experimentalist governance' (EG) in the European Union, which allows the agreement on common (but revisable) policy goals while leaving lower-level implementing units much discretion over implementation (Sabel and Zeitlin 2010). As an approach that might be able to combine rule adaptability with effective co-ordination and mutual monitoring, the EG that has been developed inside the EU might travel well to other global or international policy arenas (Campbell-Verduyn and Porter 2014; *cf.* Posner 2010).

As Campbell-Verduyn and Porter demonstrate, it is still not fully clear whether and under which circumstances that is to be expected. If, as outlined above, financial regulation in many respects continues to be a bilateral affair along the Washington–Brussels axis (or the Wall Street–City of London axis), the value-added of an institutional tool set that excels at co-ordinating a large number of actors may be limited. Should other jurisdictions, in particular China but also, for example, Mexico, become more prominent voices in global financial governance, the EU may still end up exporting EG to the global level.

In addition to being an inadvertent testing-ground for new, more fluid governance arrangements, the EU can also have the opposite effect in global governance: hardening what previously were 'soft' rules (Newman and Bach 2014). Global financial governance largely falls into the domain of 'soft law' (Brummer 2011), as agreements for example in the Basel Committee are not legally binding. That clearly distinguishes them from intra-European agreements on matters like a single supervisory mechanism. Historically, a number of global 'soft law' agreements have functioned as templates for intra-European regulations or directives, which have translated them into hard law.

This effect has ramifications beyond European borders: global soft law becomes enshrined in European law, which may in turn require, for example, firms from non-EU jurisdictions to apply these rules. Put in more general terms, because the EU itself, as a collective of member states, needs something much 'harder' than *de facto* gentlemen's agreements to govern their interactions, they end up exporting more codified versions for global agreements to the rest of the world. Just as EU countries have turned from nation states into member states (Bickerton 2012), the EU may promote the further constitutionalization – its own *modus operandi* – of financial rules on the global level (*cf.* Best 2003). That said, to what degree other jurisdictions, which face none of the EU-internal incentives for more codified interactions, will react to such developments is for the future to show.

THE FUTURE ROLE OF THE EUROPEAN UNION IN GLOBAL FINANCIAL GOVERNANCE

On the face of it, the most surprising feature of the EU's role in post-crisis global financial governance is the continuity with the pre-crisis years. The focus on international harmonization has weakened at the expense of mutual adaptation and recognition. But beyond that, we still observe international regulatory politics that bear the hallmarks of pre-crisis regulatory dynamics: competitive struggles between financial firms jockeying for regulatory advantage, and regulators trying to understand and act upon the global financial fragility that highly complex and transnationally integrated financial markets bring about. In many ways, the kinds of dynamics described by Quaglia (2014) can be expected to continue. At the same time, two major factors may significantly influence how the EU relates to the rest of the world in financial regulation: a drastic increase or decrease in internal coherence, and a new financial crisis.

The eurozone has responded to its own crisis – the 'euro crisis' – with the banking union, which not only entails a sharing of risks, for example through bank resolution arrangements and some kind of common deposit guarantee scheme, but also a single supervisory mechanism. The latter implies a centralization of competencies within the eurozone. Given the need for supervisory discretion that was evidenced by the crisis and is also clearly part of macroprudential thinking, a central eurozone supervisor cannot but be an important actor in future regulatory policy – probably at the expense of its EU-wide counterpart, the European Banking Authority. At the same time, the United Kingdom has repeatedly indicated its discontent with 'Brussels' regulatory policy, and its present premier has vowed to hold a referendum on EU membership, should he win the next election. Both of these dynamics could drastically alter how the different constituencies in the EU relate to each other and how coherent or otherwise the 'European' position in GFG will be. They also open the possibility, however, that regulatory policy from eurozone regulators, or an EU without a UK, would reflect much more the corporatist, co-ordinated policy tradition of Continental European countries.

Even more fundamentally, many observers harbour doubts as to whether the current crisis has been tackled successfully. Ultra-loose monetary policy and the asset bubbles it seems to be fuelling could still bring unwelcome surprises when the former is reined in and the latter burst. Simply put, it is not clear whether the crisis is really over, or whether it might enter another 'hot' phase in the years to come. If so, the tenuous GFG *status quo*, in which the EU's role looks much like it did before the crisis, might still be in for a fundamental disruption.

Biographical note: Daniel Mügge is a researcher at the Amsterdam Institute for Social Science Research and an associate professor at the University of Amsterdam, The Netherlands.

ACKNOWLEDGEMENTS

My own research time as well as the workshops that have led to this collection have been kindly funded by the European Commission through the FP7-funded research project GR:EEN (Global Re-ordering: Evolution through European Networks), project number 266809. The Center for European Studies at Harvard University has kindly hosted me while this particular project was set up. And I am thankful in particular to my colleague Jonathan Zeitlin, who has provided generous advice on the different contributions to this collection, as well as to Jennie Jouvenaar, who provided logistical support.

BIBLIOGRAPHY

Best, J. (2003) 'From the top–down: the new financial architecture and the re-embedding of global finance', *New Political Economy* 8(3): 363–84.

Bieling, H.-J. (2014) 'Shattered expectations: the defeat of European ambitions of global financial reform', *Journal of European Public Policy* 21(3), doi: 10.1080/13501763.2014.882969.

Bickerton, C. (2012) *From Nation States to Member States*, Oxford: Oxford University Press.

Brummer, C. (2011) *Soft Law and the Global Financial System. Rule Making in the 21st Century*, Cambridge: Cambridge University Press.

Campbell-Verduyn, M. and Porter, T. (2014) 'Experimentalism in European Union and global financial governance: interactions, contrasts, and implications', *Journal of European Public Policy* 21(3), doi: 10.1080/13501763.2014.882972.

Crouch, C. (2009) 'Privatised Keynesianism: an unacknowledged policy regime', *The British Journal of Politics & International Relations* 11(3): 382–99.

Hacker, J. and Pierson, P. (2010) 'Winner-take-all-politics. Public policy, political organization, and the percipitous rise of top incomes in the United States', *Politics & Society* 38(2): 152–204.

Hall, P. and Soskice, D. (eds) (2001) *Varieties of Capitalism: The Institutional Foundations of Comparative Advantage*, Oxford: Oxford University Press.

Helleiner, E. and Pagliari, S. (2010) 'Between the storms: patterns in global financial governance', in G. Underhill, J. Blom and D. Mügge (eds), *Global Financial Governance Thirty Years On. From Reform to Crisis*, Cambridge: Cambridge University Press, pp. 42–57.

Helleiner, E. and Pagliari, S. (2011) 'The end of an era in international financial regulation? A postcrisis research agenda', *International Organization* 65(01): 169–200.

Jayasuriya, K. (2001) 'Globalization and the changing architecture of the state: the regulatory state and the politics of negative co-ordination', *Journal of European Public Policy* 8(1): 101–23.

Moschella, M. and Tsingou, E. (eds) (2013) *Great Expectations, Slow Transformations. Incremental Change in Post-Crisis Regulation*, Colchester: ECPR Press.

Mosley, L. (2010) 'Regulating globally, implementing locally: the financial standards and codes effort', *Review of International Political Economy* 17(4): 724–61.

Mügge, D. (2013) 'Resilient neo-liberalism in European financial regulation', in V. Schmidt and M. Thatcher (eds), *Resilient Liberalism in Europe's Political Economy*, Cambridge: Cambridge University Press, pp. 201–25.

Mügge, D. and Stellinga, B. (2010) 'Insider interests and absent alternatives in post-crisis financial reform', *der moderne staat* 3(2): 321–38.

Mügge, D. (2010) *Widen the Market, Narrow the Competition. Banker Interests in the Making of a European Capital Market*, Colchester: ECPR Press.

Mügge, D. (ed.) (forthcoming) *Europe and the Governance of Global Finance*, Oxford: Oxford University Press.

Newman, A. and Bach, D. (2014) 'The European Union as hardening agent: soft law and the diffusion of global financial regulation', *Journal of European Public Policy* 21(3), doi: 10.1080/13501763.2014.882968.

Posner, E. (2010) 'The Lamfalussy Process: polyarchic origins of networked financial rulemaking in the EU', in C. Sabel and J. Zeitlin (eds), *EU Governance: Towards a New Architecture?* Oxford: Oxford University Press, pp. 43–60.

Quaglia, L. (2014) 'The sources of European Union influence in international financial regulatory fora', *Journal of European Public Policy* 21(3), doi: 10.1080/13501763.2014.882970.

Rajan, R. (2010) *Fault Lines. How Hidden Fractures Still Threaten the World Economy*, Princeton, NJ: Princeton University Press.

Sabel, C. and Zeitlin, J. (eds) (2010) *Experimentalist Governance in the European Union*, Oxford: Oxford University Press.

Seabrooke, L. and Tsingou, E. (2014) 'Distinctions, affiliations, and professional knowledge in financial reform expert groups', *Journal of European Public Policy* 21(3), doi: 10.1080/13501763.2014.882967.

Singer, D. (2007) *Regulating Capital. Setting Standards for the International Financial System*, Ithaca, NY: Cornell University Press.
The Warwick Commission on International Financial Reform (2009) *In Praise of Unlevel Playing Fields*, Coventry: University of Warwick.
Underhill, G. and Zhang, X (eds) (2003) *International Financial Governance under Stress: Global Structures versus National Imperatives*, Cambridge: Cambridge University Press.
Walter, A. (2010) 'Adopting international financial standards in Asia: convergence or divergence in the global political economy?', in G. Underhill J. Blom and D. Mügge (eds), *Global Financial Integration Thirty Years On. From Reform to Crisis*, Cambridge: Cambridge University Press, pp. 95–112.
Young, B. (2009) 'Vom staatlichen zum privatisierten Keynesianismus. Der globale makroökonomische Kontext der Finanzkrise und der Privatverschuldung', *Zeitschrift für Internationale Beziehungen* 16(1): 141–59.
Young, K. (2012) 'Transnational regulatory capture? An empirical examination of transnational lobbying of the Basel Committee on Banking Supervision', *Review of International Political Economy* 19(4): 663–88.
Young, K. (2014) 'Losing abroad but winning at home: European financial industry groups in global financial governance since the crisis', *Journal of European Public Policy* 21(3), doi: 10.1080/13501763.2014.882971.
Zysman, J. (1983) *Governments, Markets, and Growth*, Ithaca, NY: Cornell University Press.

The sources of European Union influence in international financial regulatory fora

Lucia Quaglia

ABSTRACT The European Union is one of the world's largest financial jurisdictions, and after the global financial crisis has been increasingly active in international financial regulatory fora. What affects its ability (or otherwise) to shape international financial regulation? This analysis focuses at the EU level, arguing that the cohesiveness of the EU position has greater analytical leverage than alternative explanations based on market size, regulatory capacity and representation in international fora. Empirically, the article examines a variety of case studies of low, medium and high EU influence across the main segments of the financial sector (banking, securities markets and insurance) after the global financial crisis.

1. INTRODUCTION

The European Union (EU) has become an increasingly important player in global financial regulation after what Grossman and Leblond (2011) call in the title of their article 'the great leap forward' in financial market integration in Europe. Whereas the internal dimension of EU financial regulation has been examined extensively (see Donnelly 2010; Macartney 2010; Mügge 2010; Quaglia 2010), we know relatively little about the external dimension of EU financial regulation. The few works that have examined the influence of the EU in global financial regulation have mainly done so in relation to the United States (US) (Bach and Newman 2007, 2010; Dür 2011; Posner 2010, 2009; Quaglia 2013), not with reference to international regulatory fora (for some notable exceptions see Drezner [2007]; Leblond [2011]; Mügge [2011]).

This research begins with an empirical puzzle: the degree of EU influence on international standards set by fora of national regulators in the wake of the global financial has varied across financial services. In a nutshell, it has been relatively high on insurance, medium on hedge funds and low on banking, as elaborated in the following sections. Which factors affect the influence of the EU on international standard setting? For the purpose of this research, the influence of the EU in international regulatory fora is defined as the ability of the EU to have its preferences incorporated into international standards. Unlike Mügge (2011), this research distinguishes between the influence of the EU and that of individual European countries.

In finance, unlike in trade policy (see, for example, Meunier [2005]), the EU does not have exclusive legal competences, hence the European Commission does not have the exclusive power to represent the EU and its member states in international regulatory fora. The mechanisms for the international representation of the EU and its member states vary across financial services, as detailed in the empirical sections. In several cases, the Commission participates as an observer, together with representatives from the member states, or some of them. Consequently, it is important to have a good understanding of the preferences of the main member states, in particular the United Kingdom (UK), which hosts the largest financial centre in Europe and the second largest worldwide.

It is argued that the cohesiveness of the EU position has greater analytical leverage than alternative explanations based on market size, regulatory capacity and representation in international fora. This research proceeds as follows. It first reviews theoretically informed explanations of the resources that the EU can deploy in order to influence international financial regulation. It then examines a variety of case studies of relatively high, medium and low EU influence in international standard-setting, with a view to assessing which explanations have greater analytical leverage. It concludes with an overall comparative assessment across financial services.

2. STATE OF THE ART AND RESEARCH DESIGN

The EU literature points out different resources that this regional jurisdiction can deploy in international financial regulation. First, there is 'market power' (Damro 2012; Dür 2011; see also Drezner 2007): that is the sheer size of the EU internal market. The causal mechanism is as follows. International standards are not legally binding; they become so only when they are adopted and enforced by national (or regional, in the case of the EU) jurisdictions. Consequently, the support of a jurisdiction with a large internal market is essential for the success of international standards. If a large jurisdiction decides not to comply with international standards, these standards will be substantially weakened because international fora cannot force the domestic adoption of international rules. Hence, third countries have a significant incentive to make sure that the preferences of jurisdictions with large domestic markets are taken into account in international standard-setting. Ergo, jurisdictions with large markets have greater influence than smaller jurisdictions in international regulatory fora.

The second resource that the EU can deploy in international standard-setting is its 'regulatory capacity' defined as 'a jurisdiction's ability to formulate, monitor, and enforce a set of market rules' (Bach and Newman 2007: 831).

With reference to the EU–US regulatory dialogue, Posner (2009) has operationalized this concept as regulatory centralization in the EU, which has increased the EU leverage *vis-à-vis* the US. The main causal mechanism is that a jurisdiction with regulatory centralization can preclude access to its markets to third-country firms that do not comply with its domestic rules, including those that follow international standards instead. Hence, jurisdictions with high regulatory capacity are more influential than other jurisdictions in international regulatory fora. More recently, Posner (2010) looked at the sequencing in the development of financial standards across jurisdictions, which can provide a first-mover advantage to (big) jurisdictions that first set rules in a certain sector. Here the causal mechanism is that a jurisdiction that develops regulatory templates in a certain sector is better positioned to shape international rules. Not only does it have the expertise to interact effectively in international financial regulatory fora, it also has domestic regulatory templates that can provide solutions to the regulatory issues that international standards seek to address.

Quaglia (2013) investigates the 'regulatory game' played by the EU and the US in international standard-setting in finance, focusing on the presence (or absence) of domestic 'regulatory templates'; that is, coherent sets of rules concerning certain financial activities. The presence of domestic regulatory templates concerning specific financial services creates a first-mover regulatory advantage, enabling either the EU or the US to 'upload' their rules to international fora. Yet, this account does not explain what happens when: (a) neither jurisdiction has domestic regulatory templates in place because certain financial services are subject to self-regulation (e.g., hedge funds and over the counter derivatives prior to the global financial crisis); and (b) existing templates are unfit for purpose – as demonstrated by the crisis – and new rules are needed (e.g., revised capital requirements). This is a significant blind spot because the vast majority of financial rules adopted post-crisis concerns (a) and (b).

Third, some authors have argued that the modalities of EU representation in international financial fora make a significant difference in the external influence of the EU. For example, Mügge (2011) has argued that 'European voice' is reduced when both the EU as such and the member states are represented in a given forum. Others (e.g., Hodson 2011) have argued that the mechanism for the external representation of the EU do not make much of a difference in finance.

It is noteworthy that most of the works reviewed above have overlooked the importance of the degree of 'cohesiveness' of the EU position on its influence on international financial standards. There are, however, a couple of exceptions. Adopting an approach based on varieties of capitalism and comparative political economy, Fioretos (2010; see also Zimmerman 2010) investigated the divisions across EU countries over EU and international hedge fund regulation. He criticized Drezner (2007) for just looking at market power, neglecting intra EU differences. With reference to private standard-setting, including international accounting standards, Büthe and Mattli (2011) argued that even though rule-making has shifted to the international level in several sectors, domestic regulatory institutions remain paramount. They stress the 'institutional complementarity' between the domestic and the international levels. Influence on international private standard-setting is not a function of market size, but of the ability of domestic (mainly private) standard-setters to provide timely information and speak with a single voice in international fora (Büthe and Mattli 2011: 13).

In policy areas other than international financial regulation, the cohesiveness of the EU has been considered as an important variable in order to explain its external influence. In trade policy, several works have made the rather counter-intuitive argument that where there is disunity between the member states, the EU may have more influence because the Commission is able to use domestic constraints on its bargaining position as a negotiating tool (Elgström and Frenhoff Larsén 2010; Meunier 2005; Meunier and Nicolaïdis 2006). Yet, as pointed out in the introduction, there are substantial institutional differences between trade policy and international financial regulation.

On foreign policy, some works have dealt with the EU's 'actorness' (e.g., Bretherton and Vogler 2005), which incorporates a range of factors, such as policy coherence, policy instruments, legitimacy, etc. Only a few works have examined the cohesiveness or otherwise of member state preferences and the effect this has on the EU's influence outside its borders. Some authors (e.g., Smith 2010) have argued that despite 'speaking with one voice', the EU has had limited external influence in certain international fora. Other authors have argued that the EU is more than the 'sum of its parts' and member states unity in multilateral negotiations is important for external influence (Groenleer and van Schaik 2007; van Schaik 2013).

There are two main causal mechanisms through which the cohesiveness of the EU can affect its influence in international regulatory fora. To begin with, if the EU has a cohesive stance, that is member states agree on a set of preferences, the EU will be able (*de facto*) to speak with one voice. This is the case, even if it formally does not have a single representation and the Commission does not have the power and the mandate to represent the EU. Furthermore, third countries will not be able to use the strategy of exploiting differences amongst the member states in order to weaken the EU's position in international fora. Even if third parties do not deliberately do that, intra-EU disagreement might play out in international financial regulatory fora, reducing the influence of the EU in international standard-setting.

For the sake of simplicity, this contribution considers the cohesiveness of the EU position as a spectrum that goes from a fully cohesive position (that is an EU agreement on a full set of preferences), to a loosely agreed EU position (for example, on certain principles), to the lack of a common position. The hypothesis is that the higher the cohesiveness of the EU position, the higher its influence in standard-setting. There is a positive correlation between the cohesiveness of the EU position and its regulatory capacity (Büthe and Mattli 2011), but the two concepts do not coincide. If the EU has a high degree of regulatory capacity in a given policy area, it is more likely to have a cohesive position because member state preferences have already been reconciled during intra-EU negotiations. Similarly, if the EU has a cohesive position in a certain policy area, it is more likely to have developed substantial regulatory capacity in that area because member state preferences are similar or at least compatible.

Nonetheless, the EU can have a cohesive position without (yet) having regulatory capacity, for example in policy areas or on issues that are relatively new, as in the case of hedge fund regulation examined below. The EU can also have high regulatory capacity, as in the case of banking, which was the first financial service to be regulated and integrated in the EU, but not a cohesive position on the redrafting of rules that were proven to be unfit for purpose by the crisis, as demonstrated by the different national positions on Basel III. There is also a link between cohesiveness, regulatory capacity and market size, in that the market power that derives from market size will be heavily diminished if countries express different preferences (Fioretos 2010) or if the EU does not have sufficient regulatory capacity in that market (Bach and Newman 2007).

The dependent variable studied here is the degree of EU influence on international standard-setting. For the sake of simplicity, this is conceptualized as a spectrum that goes from relatively low, to moderate and to high influence. This approach also considers the influence of individual European countries in addition to, but as distinguished from, EU influence. Influence is measured on the basis of preference attainment. If EU preferences on a certain issue are unclear, the position expressed by the European Commission in drafting the relevant legislation is considered as the EU preference.

The case studies examined in the empirical sections were selected because they vary on the dependent variable: they exemplify different degrees of EU influence in international fora, as measured by preference attainment (high, medium, low). In all the cases, the EU and/or its member states preferences were different from those of the US, which means that EU influence in preference attainment is unlikely to be confused with US influence. The empirical material was gathered through a systematic survey of policy documents and press coverage, as well as semi-structured élite interviews with policy-makers across the EU and in the US. All the interviews were conducted on non-attributable basis. Other potential case studies were considered and rejected because they did not involve fora of national regulators. For example, the International Financial Reporting Standards are issued by the International Accounting Standards Board, which is a private standard-setting body.

3. THE EU AND THE BASEL COMMITTEE ON BANKING SUPERVISION (BCBS): THE BASEL III ACCORD

The BCBS was established by the central bank governors of the Group of Ten countries in 1974. After the global financial crisis, the membership of the Committee was extended to all countries of the Group of Twenty (G20). Countries are represented by their central bank, and by the authority with formal responsibility for the prudential supervision of banking activities whenever this is not the central bank. There is no formal EU representation in the BCBS, but several EU countries are directly represented by their relevant national authorities. These are Belgium, France, Germany, Italy, Luxembourg, the Netherlands, Spain, Sweden and the United Kingdom. The European Commission and the European Central Bank (ECB) have observer status.

In banking, the most important standards concern capital requirements for banks, which were agreed for the first time by the BCBS in the Basel I accord (1988) 'International convergence of capital measurement and capital standards'. This was replaced in 2005 by the Basel II accord, which was followed by the Basel III accord (BCBS 2010a, b) in the wake of the global financial crisis. The content of these accords has periodically been incorporated by the EU into the capital requirements directives. Other jurisdictions also incorporated it into their national law. For example, Basel I was implemented in more than 100 countries.

The Basel III accord was a crucial piece of regulation adopted in response to the global financial crisis. Its blueprint was outlined by the BCBS in September 2009 and the final version of the accord was eventually signed in December 2010 (BCBS 2010a, b). The Basel III accord provides a (rather restrictive) definition of what counts as capital; increases the risk weight of several assets (e.g., the trading book); introduces capital buffers; sets up a leverage ratio; and outlines international rules on liquidity management. The Basel III rules will be phased in gradually from January 2013 until 2019.[1]

The Basel III accord provides for the first time a common definition of capital, on which there had been no agreement in the past. In particular, it bans the use of double counting of capital for bancassurance (that is banks with significant insurance activities) and phases out the use of 'hybrid capital' (BCBS 2010a: 2), that is instruments that have features of securities and debt. This narrow definition of capital was advocated by the US and the UK, where bank capital is mainly constituted of shares. It was resisted by continental policy-makers because the phasing out of certain capital instruments would considerably reduce the capital base of many European banks (*The Economist* 2010; interviews, Brussels, March 2012).

Whereas the US and the UK were keen to set higher capital requirements, continental European regulators somewhat reluctantly agreed to this (*Financial Times* 2010 a, b, c). A similar division emerged on the 'leverage ratio', which is a non-risk-based leverage ratio calibrated to act as a supplementary measure to the risk-based capital requirements. This regulatory instrument was already used in the US, but was opposed by continental European countries (interviews, Frankfurt, June 2011; Paris, June 2011), whose banks were overleveraged and would therefore encounter serious difficulties in complying with a leverage ratio.

Likewise, the US and the UK supported the establishment of internationally harmonized minimum liquidity standards (BCBS 2010a: 8–9), whereas continental European states were reluctant to endorse them. One point of contention was which categories of financial instruments should be considered as liquid (interview, Paris, May 2011).[2] The UK was the first country to introduce unilateral liquidity requirements after the crisis. The US also had liquidity rules already in place, whereas for many continental banks it would have been difficult to meet the new rules.

More generally, continental regulators were worried about the potential impacts of the new rules on lending (interviews, Paris, July 2011; Frankfurt, July 2011; Brussels, June 2011), in particular in bank-based continental financial systems, where banks are the main source of finance for firms, especially for small and medium enterprises. The prolonged phased in period of many Basel III provisions is explained by these concerns. For example, at the crucial meeting of the BCBS in September 2010, prior to the agreement reached in December 2010, German policy-makers refused to endorse the document prepared by the BCBS, asking for and subsequently obtaining a longer transition period (interview, Frankfurt, April 2012; see BCBS 2010c).

Overall, the negotiations of the Basel III accord were characterized by a division between, on the one side, the US, the UK and Switzerland, which had been hardly hit by the financial crisis and were keen to impose a stricter definition of capital as well as higher capital requirements and liquidity rules. On the other side, continental European countries, first and foremost Germany, France and Italy, were reluctant to accept these rules. The Commission, which had observer status in the BCBS, attempted to co-ordinate the positions of national financial regulators from EU countries sitting in the Committee. For example, prior to the meeting in Basel, there were periodical (but not Basel-specific) meetings of the European Banking Committee and the Economic and Financial Committee (interview, Brussels, June 2011). Despite the Commission's effort, the EU lacked a cohesive position during the Basel III negotiations: European regulators pursued different preferences concerning the content and the implementation period of the new rules. These preferences were rooted in domestic political economies, in particular the configuration of national banking sectors and the link bank industry (for a comparative political economy analysis of Basel III, see Howarth and Quaglia [2013]). On several important issues the financial industry was divided along national lines (Buckley *et al.* 2012).

In this instance, it is rather problematic to measure EU influence by using preference attainment because the EU did not have an agreed position in the BCBS. For this reason, the European Commission's proposal for the implementation of Basel III in the EU through a directive that governs the access to deposit-taking activities (European Commission 2011a) and a regulation that establishes prudential requirements for credit institutions (European Commission 2011b) is considered as the EU preference. The fact that this proposal, which was issued a few months after Basel III had been agreed, was rather different from what was agreed by the BCBS (International Monetary Fund 2011) suggests that the EU was not satisfied with the international standards.

The Commission 'softened' the definition of Core Tier I capital relative to the Basel III rules. Notably, the Commission draft allowed 'silent participations', that is state loans that make up a significant part of the capital of many EU banks. The Commission's draft limited the role of the leverage ratio designed to limit risk-taking at banks. On liquidity, the Commission adopted a less prescriptive definition of liquid assets for the liquidity coverage ratio. Finally, the Commission's draft lacked a firm commitment to implement the net stable funding ratio by 2018 called for in Basel III (Howarth and Quaglia 2013).

In the Basel III negotiations, the EU lacked a cohesive position: national regulators from Europe 'batted for themselves and their financial industry' (interview, Washington, August 2011). The EU, as such, had a relatively low influence on the international standards issued, and attempted to modify them substantially through EU legislation. By 2010, the EU had centralized its regulatory capacity in banking (as well as in other financial services); it had a banking sector larger than the US, and the Commission and the ECB sat as observer in the BCBS (the ECB also chaired in that period). Yet, this did not make much of a difference on the EU's influence, given the fact that the EU, despite efforts from the Commission, could not agree on what it wanted with reference to the new rules.

4. THE EU AND THE INTERNATIONAL ASSOCIATION OF INSURANCE SUPERVISORS (IAIS): THE INTERNATIONAL SOLVENCY STANDARDS

The IAIS was established in 1993 and encompasses more than 100 national jurisdictions, including the vast majority of EU member states. The European Commission is a member of the IAIS, without voting power. Unlike in the IOSCO, the USA does not have a predominant influence in the IAIS (Singer 2007). In the US, insurance is entirely a state competence, not a federal competence, unlike securities, which is a federal competence, and banking, which is a dual (state and federal) competence. In the IAIS, the US is represented by the NAIC and 56 jurisdictions. The National Association of Insurance Commissioners (NAIC) is not a federal regulatory body, hence is often unable to project a unified US position in the IAIS and cannot guarantee uniformity and consistency in the domestic implementation of internationally agreed rules (Singer 2007). Insurance regulation is quite outdated in the US. Attempts, for example by the NAIC, to transfer regulatory competence to the federal level and to modernize the legislation, were short-lived (see the Solvency Modernization Initiative in 2008).[3]

In 2007, the EU passed the so-called Solvency II directive that set in place a state of the art financial regulation, giving 'European companies a head start in the global economy', whereas the US 'was stuck with highly fragmented insurance regulation' (*Financial Times* 2007). EU legislation adopts the concept of enterprise risk management (ERM) and relies on market valuation of assets and liabilities. It envisages the use of internal model of insurers to calculate capital requirements and relies on targeting solvency capital to specific confidence levels. Finally, EU legislation establishes group supervision, to be performed by colleges of supervisors. The EU model of solvency requirements embodied in the Solvency II directive differs widely from the regulatory model in place in the US in the three respects mentioned above. In the US the valuation of assets and liabilities is based on principles and rules, the use of internal model is not allowed and there is no group calculation of solvency requirements and group supervision.

It is remarkable that key topics of the IAIS regulatory agenda from the mid-2000s onwards – namely 'enterprise risk management', 'structure of regulatory capital'; 'use of internal models'; 'group supervision'; 'mutual recognition of supervisory regimes' – very much reflected EU priorities and perspectives (interview, Basel, November 2008), not the US regulatory model. Key concepts of the Solvency II approach – such as the ERM, market valuation of assets and liabilities, technical provisions, calibration of solvency capital to specific confidence levels, choice of internal model or standardized model, group supervision – found their way into IAIS standards and guidelines. The IAIS's guidance paper on principles of group-wide supervision borrowed from the group regime painstakingly negotiated in the Solvency II directive. These papers eventually made their way into the 'Insurance core principles, standards, guidance and assessment methodology' (IAIS 2013)

The IAIS paper on mutual recognition (2008) provided guidance on cross-border recognition of reinsurance supervision with a view to convince the US to abolish its regime for alien (non-US) insurers. The purpose of the IAIS guidance was 'to allow a supervisor to recognize the value of the supervision exercised by another jurisdiction and thus remove significant amounts of unnecessary regulatory and supervisory requirements for reinsurers' (IAIS 2008: 1). Reportedly, the Commission and the UK representatives were instrumental in pushing this issue onto the IAIS agenda, given the fact that the main international reinsurers are headquartered in the EU, first and foremost in London (interviews, London, September 2008). British officials chaired the relevant committees for the preparatory work at the IAIS (i.e., the sub-committee on solvency) and in the EU (the so-called Sharma group, named after the British official who chaired it). Reportedly, the European Commission's representative sitting in the IAIS, who also followed the dossier on Solvency II in the EU, was very active in the IAIS.

In this case, unlike in Basel III, the EU had a relatively high influence in international standard setting in insurance, as compared to the US (interview, Washington, August 2011). The EU (to be precise, the Commission and the EU member states in the IAIS) presented a rather cohesive position based on the (then newly agreed) EU solvency rules. Unlike in Basel III, the preferences of the main EU member states on important features of the risk-based solvency regime were similar: these countries host the headquarters of large insurance companies, which were deemed to benefit from the Solvency II rules (CEA 2007). Particularly important is the fact that on the key issues the priorities of the UK coincided with those of the main continental countries. By contrast, the US was unable to project a cohesive position in the IAIS: there was turf fighting between the NAIC and state regulators, and state insurance regulation varied somewhat across the US (Quaglia 2013).

Solvency II endowed the EU with considerable regulatory capacity, in particular the centralization of regulatory authority, which the EU projected internationally as well as bilaterally, for example on equivalence decisions,[4] as suggested by the EU–US regulatory dialogue in insurance that began in 2011. Prior to that date, the US had felt no need for such a dialogue with the EU. EU influence was facilitated by the weak US regulatory capacity in this field, its fragmented system of external representation in the IAIS and the participation of the European Commission to this forum. The EU and US have almost the same market size in insurance, hence market power does not seem to have much explanatory leverage.

5. THE EU AND THE INTERNATIONAL ORGANIZATION OF SECURITIES COMMISSIONS (IOSCO): PRINCIPLES ON HEDGE FUNDS REGULATION

The IOSCO was established in 1983 and its membership encompasses more than 100 national jurisdictions. No EU representative as such sits in the IOSCO. Unlike in the IAIS, the influence of the US Securities and Exchanges Commission (SEC) has been predominant in the IOSCO because of its strong domestic regulatory capacity and cutting edge expertise (Bach and Newman 2010).

After the global financial crisis, the IOSCO, under the political impetus of the G20, expanded substantially its regulatory remit. One of the most controversial new areas of regulation concerned hedge funds. Prior to the crisis, some continental countries, first and foremost Germany and France, had called for international hedge fund regulation in international fora. By contrast, the US and the UK, which host the majority of hedge fund managers worldwide, resisted it (Fioretos 2010; Helleiner and Pagliari 2009). In the EU, the UK had also resisted any Franco-German attempt to include hedge funds into the scope of EU legislation. Impasse followed, and no regulatory action was undertaken either by the IOSCO or by the EU with reference to hedge funds. Pagliari notes that 'the US SEC endorsed IOSCO's minimal approach towards the regulation of market actors such as a rating agencies and hedge funds' (Pagliari 2011).

Prior to the crisis, the EU lacked a cohesive position: the European Commission was not keen on the idea of regulating hedge funds (in the EU or internationally) and the member states had difference preferences, rooted in domestic political economy, namely different configuration of the financial system and national varieties of capitalism (Zimmermann 2010). Whereas the UK hosts the vast majority of hedge fund managers in the EU, Germany and especially France host many assets managers, which on certain business compete with hedge fund managers (Woll 2013). Moreover, the activity of hedge funds was regarded as challenging corporate governance arrangements on the continent (Quaglia 2011). Finally, partly for the reasons just mentioned, hedge funds and/or fund managers in some continental countries were subject to more prescriptive regulation than in the UK and, unlike in insurance, an EU regulatory template was missing on hedge funds.

In the wake of the global financial crisis, several European countries, led by France and Germany (see Sarkozy's and Merkel's joint letter of 2009)[5] pushed for a tougher regulatory regime for hedge funds internationally and in the EU. The UK shifted its position closer to continental countries and so did the European Commission, hence the EU presented a rather cohesive position at the G20 London summit in April 2009. The convergence of the UK towards the French and German position on the need to regulate hedge funds is more important than the international consensus on the need to reform the Basel rules, because in the past the UK had forcefully opposed the regulation of hedge funds, blocking any proposal for EU and international rules.

Prior to the G20 summit, the European Council, under the aegis of the German Chancellor, agreed on the principle that 'all financial markets, products and participants must be subject to appropriate oversight or regulation, without exception and regardless of their country of domicile. This is especially true for those private pools of capital, including hedge funds, that may present a systemic risk.'[6] This important principle found its way, after protracted negotiations, into the G20 agreement in London in April 2009. The G20 agreement, which was followed by the expansion of the IOSCO perimeter of regulation to hedge funds (and other previously unregulated or self-regulated activities, such as over the counter derivatives), could be seen as evidence of EU influence. However, the US had also switched position in favour of hedge funds regulation for domestic politics reasons, namely the public backlash against financial institutions and the politicization of financial regulation (Helleiner and Pagliari 2009).

In the IOSCO, the Task Force on Unregulated Financial Entities, co-chaired by the Italian securities markets authority (CONSOB) and the British Financial Services Authority (FSA), decided to focus its work on hedge funds. The task force was chaired by two regulatory agencies embracing very different domestic regulatory models about hedge funds. The Report Hedge Funds Oversight produced by the Task Force was published for consultation in March 2009. The Final Report (IOSCO 2009), published in June 2009, recommended six high-level principles. Amongst the most important: 'Hedge funds and/or hedge fund managers/advisers should be subject to mandatory registration.' 'Hedge fund managers/advisers which are required to register should also be subject to appropriate ongoing regulatory requirements'. 'Hedge fund managers/advisers and prime brokers should provide to the relevant regulator information for systemic risk purposes.' (extracts from IOSCO 2009: 8).

Overall, the report (IOSCO 2009) is a rather bland document. Indeed, it is deliberately ambiguous on the rather crucial issue of whether certain provisions should apply to hedge funds or hedge funds managers. Regulators in Italy, Germany and France, where hedge funds, and not only hedge funds managers, are subject to registration and/or supervisory oversight, were in favour of regulating the hedge fund, not just the fund manager. They also called for more prescriptive prudential requirements, somewhat akin to those for banks or regulated funds. In contrast, the UK and the US (and the hedge funds industry) wanted to limit the application of the IOSCO principles to hedge fund managers and opposed certain prudential requirements.

The EU lacked a cohesive position on the content of the IOSCO standards: European regulators articulated different preferences and the Commission was not represented in the IOSCO. In the same period, the EU was negotiating, but had not yet agreed, the Directive on Alternative Investment Fund Managers (AIFMs), which mainly target hedge fund managers and private equities managers. The European Commission held a public consultation in December 2008, the feedback from this consultation was discussed at a high-level conference in Brussels in late February 2009. The directive was officially proposed by the European Commission in April 2009 and is considered as the EU preference on hedge funds regulation, even though the scope of the directive was broader than the scope of the work of the IOSCO Task Force. The proposed directive had the objective of creating a comprehensive and effective regulatory and supervisory framework for AIFMs in the EU. It contained provisions on the leverage employed by hedge fund managers, imposed minimum capital requirements, as well as valuation and depository requirements.

Intra EU negotiations on the AIFM directive were contested because the hedge fund industry opposed strict rules. Moreover, the main European countries had different preferences on issues such as third-country access to the EU market and prudential requirements – this was for reasons related to domestic political economy (Buckley and Howarth 2011). Some divisions amongst European regulators, for example on prudential requirements, emerged in the EU as well as the IOSCO. In parallel, the US was also discussing the revision of its hedge fund regulation, as part of the Dodd Frank Act. Pagliari (2011) notes that the act was largely in line with the IOSCO standards (and in some cases it fell short of them).

Overall, the record of EU influence in international standards for hedge funds was mixed. Prior to the crisis, the EU lacked a cohesive position and member states had competing preferences. The UK and the US successfully opposed any attempt to directly include hedge funds (or fund managers) in the perimeter of international regulation. After the crisis, there was a realignment of preferences within the EU, and the EU reached a cohesive position on the principle of regulating hedge funds. Under the aegis of France and Germany, the EU was highly influential in getting hedge funds into the international regulatory agenda. This outcome was facilitated by the changed preferences of the UK and the US and their somewhat weakened positions after the global financial crisis, which originated in the States and hit the UK very badly. However, when the international standards were negotiated by the IOSCO, the EU lacked a cohesive position on the specific content of regulation (intra-EU negotiations were ongoing), hence its influence in shaping those standards was limited.

The market size for hedge funds can be defined by the assets under management of managers located in the EU and the US. The amount of assets under management by US-based hedge fund managers is significantly larger than in the EU. In terms of regulatory capacity, the EU was in the process of building up its regulatory template (the AIFM directive). The EU as such was not represented in IOSCO, where the European Commission, which proposed the AIFM directive, was not a member. This is likely to have hampered the EU ability to project its regulatory preferences internationally.

6. AN OVERALL ASSESSMENT ACROSS SECTORS AND OVER TIME

The influence of the EU in international regulatory fora varies across financial services and policy episodes. In all the case studies examined, the preferences of the EU were different from those of the US. Hence, preference attainment is a good indicator of EU influence (or the lack of it), in particular when compared to the US. In Basel III, the EU had a relatively low influence, but the main European countries managed to have some of their distinctive preferences included in the accord. In the embryonic solvency standards discussed by the IAIS, the EU had relatively high influence, with the caveats that the standard-setting process is ongoing. The international principles for hedge funds regulation issued by the IOSCO are a case of medium EU influence: such influence concerned the principle of extending the perimeter of regulation to hedge funds, rather than the specific content of international standards.

What affects EU influence across financial services and policy episodes? The cohesiveness of the EU position is the main explanatory variable for the influence of the EU in international standard setting, as in the case of solvency standards for insurers and extending the scope of regulation to hedge funds. In both episodes, UK policy-makers sided with continental ones – this was crucial for EU cohesiveness. Furthermore, the relatively high influence of the EU in the IAIS was facilitated by the lack of a cohesive US position on solvency standards.

In many financial services nowadays the EU has the same market size as its main counterpart, the US. Hence, market size cannot account for variations in EU influence across services. Indeed, the EU, which has the largest banking sector in the world, had limited influence on Basel III because it lacked a cohesive position. Market size is a necessary condition for international influence, but it is not a sufficient one. Regulatory capacity does not have great explanatory power in the post crisis period, when the EU (and other jurisdictions) lacked regulatory templates on certain financial services, or existing regulatory templates had clearly failed and needed to be reformed. The external representation of the EU in this area, in particular whether the Commission is included (or not) a given international regulatory fora, seem to be a facilitating (but not crucial) factor for EU influence (Hodson 2011). This was the case of the participation of the Commission to the IAIS and its absence in the IOSCO, but did not make much of a difference in the case of the BCBS, where the ECB was also present.

What explains the cohesiveness or otherwise of EU position across financial services and policy episode? Since the EU institutional framework dealing with financial regulation is the same for all financial services, institutional explanations do not have much explanatory mileage, unlike for example in trade policy (*cf.* Meunier 2005). The main explanation is based on convergent (or at least compatible) preferences of the member states (Moravcsik 1993, 1998), rooted in the domestic political economy of financial services regulation (see Busch 2004).

In the case of capital requirements for banks, the configuration of the national banking sector and the link bank–industry account for the different preferences of the member state and the non-cohesive EU position (Buckley *et al.* 2012). The UK banking system is highly internationalized, banks are well capitalized and provide limited credit to the domestic real economy. French banks have an important international profile, but retain a strong domestic presence. Like German banks they are not well capitalized and rely on domestic retail banking. The German financial system is both the least concentrated in Europe and the least internationalized of the three. There are thousands of undercapitalized public and small local banks which provide the bulk of funding to, and maintain close relations with, small and medium enterprises (Howarth and Quaglia 2013). For these reasons, the banking industry in the EU lacked a cohesive position on Basel III; it mostly split along national lines.

In insurance, the main member states shared similar preferences because the configurations of their national insurance industries were similar. In particular, the big insurance players in the main member states were deemed to benefit from the new solvency requirements set by the EU in the 2000s. According to the European Commission, the new rules would allow large insurance groups to save up to 40 per cent of their solvency requirements, freeing vast sums up for profitable investments (*Financial Times* 2007). The smaller insurers got some exemptions. Hence, the insurance industry had a rather cohesive position on solvency requirements in the EU and internationally.

In the case of hedge funds, the fact that the UK hosts two-thirds of hedge fund managers in Europe explains why it was reluctant to subject them to heavy regulation (Buckley and Howarth 2011). By contrast, the main continental countries already had prescriptive national rules in place and a variety of capitalism in which hedge funds were not embedded. Moreover, France hosted the heavily regulated assets management industry, which often competed for business with hedge funds (Woll 2013). Whereas hedge fund managers had a rather cohesive position against regulation, asset managers were in favour of hedge funds regulation.

There might be two additional variables to be considered in this explanation.[7] The first variable is whether the EU operates in international regulatory fora trying to promote new international standards or tries to oppose standards proposed by the US or other jurisdictions. The literature on lobbying suggests that

Table 1 An overview of the research design applied to the case studies

International standards and standard setting bodies	*Basel III (2010) BCBS*	*Solvency standards (2011) IAIS*	*Hedge funds principles (2011) IOSCO*
Independent variable 1: cohesiveness of EU position	No	Yes	Yes, but only on principles
Independent variable 2: EU market size	EU>US	EU=US	US>EU
Independent variable 3: EU regulatory capacity	EU rules ad US rules unfit for purpose	EU state of the art rules, outdated US rules	EU and US rules in the making (at that time)
Dependent variable: EU influence	Relatively low, but European countries influence	Relatively high	Intermediate, on principles rather than content
External variable: preferences US	Different from EU/European member states	Different from EU/European member states	Some agreement EU-US on principles, but differences on content

the degree of cohesiveness in the preferences of different groups is less important in influencing their influence when these groups are trying to veto a legislative proposal (Mahoney 2008). In all the case studies, the EU was not a veto player. Even in Basel III, the EU supported new capital rules, but different European countries had different preferences about the specific content of some of these rules.

The other potential missing variables are the preferences and the cohesiveness of the US. In all the three cases, the US and the EU had different preferences. On the one hand, it is true that the case in which the EU had the greatest influence was where the US was less cohesive: that is, insurance. On the other hand, in the case in which the EU had the lowest influence, namely Basel III, the US was represented in the BCBS by no less than four regulatory agencies, which did not help in forming a cohesive position (one senior treasury official remarked that 'the only time US regulators were united in the Basel III negotiations was to go against the US treasury').

7. CONCLUSIONS

This contribution set out to examine the sources of EU influence in international regulatory fora in finance. The main finding is that the degree of cohesiveness of EU position has greater explanatory power than market size and regulatory capacity for post-crisis financial regulation. Particularly important for the EU cohesiveness is whether the UK sides with the US or the rest of the EU (first and foremost, France and Germany).

This research has focused on the influence of the EU in the international standard-setting by international regulatory fora. However, the EU can influence international financial regulation in other ways. After the crisis, the EU has issued new legislation containing so-called 'equivalence' clauses that have the practical effects of encouraging third countries to change their domestic rules so as to make them equivalent to EU rules, or increase the cost for thirdcountry firms to provide services in the EU, subjecting them to EU requirements in addition to their home regulation. Moreover, the EU can influence standard setting in private bodies. During and after the global financial crisis, the EU has put a considerable amount of pressure on the IASB, calling for the reform its governance structure and the revision of its mark-to-market accounting rules (Leblond 2011). These are all interesting venues for further research.

Biographical note: Lucia Quaglia is professor of political science at the University of York.

ACKNOWLEDGEMENTS

Lucia Quaglia wishes to acknowledge financial support from the European Research Council (Grant 204398 FINGOVEU), and the British Academy and the Leverhulme Trust (SG 120191). This contribution was written while she was visiting fellow at the European University Institute and Hanse WissenschaftsKolleg. I wish the thank the editors, the anonymous reviewers, the particiants to the workshops held at the University of Amsterdam in February 2013 and the research seminar at the University of Bremen in April 2013.

NOTES

1 The discussion on Basel III draws on Howarth and Quaglia (2013).
2 For example, the French authorities opposed the use of public bonds as sole instruments of liquidity (interview, Paris, July 2011).
3 See http://www.naic.org/index_smi.htm (accessed February 2014).
4 The European Commission was given the task of assessing which third countries have an insurance regime equivalent to Solvency II and would not be required to hold additional capital.
5 Letter sent jointly by M. Nicolas Sarkozy, President of the Republic of France, and Ms Angela Merkel, Chancellor of Germany, to M. Mirek Topolanek, Prime Minister of the Czech Republic and Jose Manuel Barroso President of the European

Commission, Paris, 16 March 2009. Available at http://ambafrance-us.org/spip.php?article1281 (accessed February 2014).

6 http://uk.reuters.com/article/2009/02/22/uk-g20-europe-sb-idUKTRE51L19Y20090222 (accessed May 2010).

7 I wish to thank a reviewer for this point.

REFERENCES

Bach, D. and Newman, A.L. (2007) 'The European regulatory state and global public policy: micro-institutions, macro-influence', *Journal of European Public Policy* 14(6): 827–46.

Bach, D. and Newman, A.L. (2010) 'Transgovernmental networks and domestic policy convergence: evidence from insider trading regulation', *International Organisation* 64: 505–28.

Basel Committee of Banking Supervision (BCBS) (2010a) 'Basel III: a global regulatory framework for more resilient banks and banking systems', December, Basel.

Basel Committee of Banking Supervision (BCBS) (2010b) 'Basel III: international framework for liquidity risk measurement, standards and monitoring', December, Basel.

Basel Committee of Banking Supervision (BCBS) (2010c) 'Group of governors and heads of supervision announces higher global minimum capital standards', 12 September, Basel.

Bretherton, C. and Vogler, J. (2005) *The European Union as a Global Actor*, London: Routledge.

Buckley, J. and Howarth, D. (2011) 'Regulating the so-called "vultures of capitalism"', *Journal of Common Market Studies*, 49(s1): 123–43.

Buckley, J., Howarth, D. and Quaglia, L. (2012) 'Internal market: the ongoing struggle to 'protect' Europe from its money men', *Journal of Common Market Studies*, Annual Review 48(s 1): 119–41.

Busch, A. (2004) 'National filters: Europeanisation, institutions, and discourse in the case of banking regulation', *West European Politics*, 27(2): 310–33.

Büthe, T. and Mattli, W. (2011) *The New Global Rulers: The Privatization of Regulation in the World Economy*, Princeton, NJ: Princeton University Press.Br

Comite' Europe'en des Assurances (CEA) (2007) 'The insurance groups and Solvency II', *Briefing Note 2 May*. Brussels.

Damro, C. (2012) 'Market power Europe', *Journal of European Public Policy* 19(5): 682–99.

Donnelly, S. (2010) *The Regimes of European Integration*, Oxford: Oxford University Press.

Drezner, D.W. (2007) *All Politics is Global: Explaining International Regulatory Regimes*, Princeton, NJ: Princeton University Press.

Dür, A. (2011) 'Fortress Europe or open door Europe? The external impact of the EU's single market in financial services', *Journal of European Public Policy* 45(5): 771–87.

Elgström, O. and Frenhoff Larsén, M. (2010) 'Free to trade? Commission autonomy in the Economic Partnership Agreement negotiations', *Journal of European Public Policy* 17(2): 205–23.

European Commission (2011a) 'Proposal for a directive on the access to the activity of credit institutions and the prudential supervision of credit institutions and investment firms', COM (2011) 453 Final, 20 July, Brussels: Commission of the European Communities.

European Commission (2011b) 'Proposal for a regulation on prudential requirements for credit institutions and investment firms', COM (2011) 452 Final, 20 July, Brussels: Commission of the European Communities.

Financial Times (2007) 'EU insurance shift "will hit US"', 11 July, p. 8.

Financial Times (2010a) 'Fears for German banks under new rules', 10 September, p. 21.
Financial Times (2010b) 'International economy: a display of disunity', 22 October, p. 9.
Financial Times (2010c) 'King calls for radical bank reforms', 26 October, p. 2.
Fioretos, K.O. (2010) 'Capitalist diversity and the international regulation of hedge funds', *Review of International Political Economy* 17(3): 696–723.
Groenleer, M.L. P. and van Schaik, L.G. (2007) 'United we stand? The European Union's international actorness in the cases of the International Criminal Court and Kyoto Protocol', *Journal of Common Market Studies* 45(5): 969–98.
Grossman, E. and Leblond, P. (2011) 'European financial integration: finally the great leap forward?', *Journal of Common Market Studies* 49(2): 413–35.
Helleiner, E. and Pagliari, S. (2009) 'The end of self-regulation? Hedge funds and derivatives in global financial governance', in E. Helleiner, S. Pagliari and H. Zimmermann (eds), *Global Finance in Crisis, The Politics of International Regulatory Change*, London: Routledge, pp. 74–90.
Hodson, D. (2011) *Governing the Euro Area in Good Times and Bad*, Oxford: Oxford University Press.
Howarth, D. and Quaglia, L. (2013) 'Banking on stability: the political economy of new capital requirements in the European Union', *Journal of European Integration* 35(3): 333–46.
International Association of Insurance Supervisors (IAIS) (2008) 'Guidance paper no. 3.5 on the mutual recognition of reinsurance supervision', Basel, 17 October.
International Association of Insurance Supervisors (IAIS) (2013) *Insurance Core Principles, Standards, Guidance and Assessment Methodology, 1 October 2011; ICP 9 Amended 12 October 1012; ICP 22 Amended 19 October 2013*, available at http://www.iaisweb.org/view/element_href.cfm?src=1/20567.pdf (accessed February 2014).
International Monetary Fund (2011) 'United Kingdom: staff report for the 2011 Article IV consultation – supplementary information', IMF Country Report No. 11/220, July. Washington, DC.
International Organization of Securities Commissions (IOSCO) (2009) 'Final report on hedge funds oversight', June, Madrid.
Leblond, P. (2011) 'EU, US and international accounting standards: a delicate balancing act in governing global finance', *Journal of European Public Policy* 18(3): 443–61.
Macartney, H. (2010) *Variegated Neoliberalism: EU Varieties of Capitalism and International Political Economy*, London: Routledge.
Mahoney, C. (2008) *Brussels vs the Beltway: Advocacy in the United States and the European Union*, Washington, DC: Georgetown University Press.
Meunier, S. (2005) *Trading Voices: The European Union in International Commercial Negotiations*, Princeton, NJ: Princeton University Press.
Meunier, S. and Nicolaïdis, K. (2006) 'The European Union as a conflicted trade power', *Journal of European Public Policy* 13(6): 906–25.
Moravcsik, A. (1993) 'Preferences and power in the European Community: a liberal intergovernmental approach', *Journal of Common Market Studies* 31(4): 473–524.
Moravcsik, A. (1998) *The Choice For Europe*, London: University College London Press.
Mügge, D.K. (2010) *Widen the Market, Narrow the Competition: Banker Interests and the Making of a European Capital Market*, Colchester: European Consortium of Political Research.
Mügge, D.K. (2011) 'The European presence in global financial governance: a principal–agent perspective', *Journal of European Public Policy* 18(3): 383–402.

Pagliari, S. (2011) 'Who governs finance? The shifting public–private divide in the regulation of derivatives, rating agencies and hedge funds', *European Law Journal* 18(1): 44–61.

Posner, E. (2009) 'Making rules for global finance: transatlantic regulatory cooperation at the turn of the millennium', *International Organisation* 63: 665–99.

Posner, E. (2010) 'Sequence as explanation: the international politics of accounting standards', *Review of International Political Economy* 14(4): 639–64.

Quaglia, L. (2010) *Governing Financial Services in the European Union*, London: Routledge.

Quaglia, L. (2011) 'The "old" and "new" political economy of hedge funds regulation in the European Union', *West European Politics* 34(4): 665–82.

Quaglia, L. (2013) 'The European Union, the USA and international standard setting in finance', *New Political Economy*, doi:10.1080/13563467.2013.796449.

Singer, D.A. (2007) *Regulating capital: Setting Standards for the International Financial System*, Ithaca, NY: Cornell University Press.

Smith, K.E. (2010) 'The European Union at the Human Rights Council: speaking with one voice but having little influence', *Journal of European Public Policy* 17(2): 224–41.

van Schaik, L. (2013) *EU Effectiveness and Unity in Multilateral Negotiations: More Than The Sum of its Parts?* Basingstoke: Palgrave Macmillan.

Woll, C. (2013) 'Lobbying under pressure: the effect of salience on European Union hedge fund regulation', *Journal of Common Market Studies* 51(3): 555–72.

Zimmermann, H. (2010), 'Varieties of global financial governance? British and German approaches to financial market regulation', in E. Helleiner, S. Pagliari and H. Zimmerman (eds), *Global Finance in Crisis*, London: Routledge, pp. 121–38.

Shattered expectations: the defeat of European ambitions of global financial reform

Hans-Jürgen Bieling

ABSTRACT As a consequence of the global financial crisis, many observers expected that the European Union would initiate and spur the reform of global finance. However, it turned out that the European endeavours have only been modest and unassertive so far. This contribution aims to explore this development. It argues that there are various causes of the European defeat, but that it is possible to identify some structural factors which enabled powerful political actors to defend a liberally organized financial market environment: externally, international communication and bargaining processes have been and still are structurally biased towards a liberal global financial order owing to the strong role of global financial centres and the dynamics of competitive deregulation; and internally, the emergence of a new European economy, based on financial market integration and manifold processes of financialization, has brought about fundamental changes of European capitalism as well as of societal and intergovernmental power relations.

1. INTRODUCTION

In the period following the outbreak of the American 'subprime crisis', there was a clear renunciation of the former European public discourse on the superior economic performance of capital market based capitalist models. Leading European politicians such as Angela Merkel and Nicolas Sarkozy (Barber *et al.* 2008; Hall *et al.* 2009), but also many journalists and academics became critical of Anglo-American capitalism while praising its counterpart, the so-called 'Rhenish model'. In view of the crisis-prone nature, the short-term orientation and the high public costs of strongly financialized capitalist systems, it was quite common to emphasize the necessity of bringing finance under political control again in order to allow companies to modernize more smoothly and become long-term oriented. This overall view was not only prevalent in the media. It also took hold in open-minded scholarly debates, among regulatory experts and influential policy circles (Baker 2013). While a whole range of political statements nourished ambitious expectations of comprehensive financial re-regulation, quite a few academic contributions took these proclamations fairly literally. They assumed that the transition towards a new a phase of re-embedding global finance had been initiated (Germain 2009; Nesvetailova and Palan 2010), and for many observers it seemed obvious that the European Union (EU) would represent an important political force in this process (Moschella 2011; Posener 2010).

Although there have been and still are a lot of re-regulatory activities in the financial field, they fall short of the far-reaching expectations of that time. Overall, the nature of change was not fundamental and comprehensive but only gradual and piecemeal, i.e., based on a series of limited and very issue specific regulations (Baker 2013; Rixen 2013). Most scholars attribute the modest outcome of regulatory initiatives to the distinctive features of individual financial segments and types of actors which correspond with different national models and priorities of European capitalist development (Buckley and Howarth 2010; Hall 2012; Zimmermann 2010) and a still fragmented institutional nature of the EU in terms of global and European economic governance (Dür and Elsig 2011; Hervé 2012; Quaglia 2012; Rommerskirchen 2013; Smith 2012). The aim of this contribution is not to fundamentally question the insights offered by the prevailing institutionalist accounts. Without doubt, their focus on the role of particular actors within the given institutional setting is quite telling. At the same time, however, institutionalist views tend to neglect that the interplay of actors and institutions is strongly influenced by the specific – transnational – mode of capitalist reproduction and societal power relations. To take these dimensions into account, this contribution strives to reformulate some of the institutionalist findings by placing them into a wider political economic context. Such a politico-economically based approach seems conceptually auspicious in two regards: first, it not only looks at the fragmented or unitary nature of European and global political actors in governance but also traces their eventual bargaining capabilities to the structural power given by the respective modes of capitalist development; and second, it seems to be more sensitive in terms of the mutual – however asymmetrical – economic and financial interdependence of national capitalist models, as well as the transnational networks which both represent core elements of the 'interactive embeddedness' (Seabrooke 2001: 3) of European and global financial market policies.

Based on such a broadened politico-economic perspective, this contribution aims to explore the causes of the defeat of more far-reaching European reform ambitions. It argues that they are various, but that it is possible to identify some structural – politically mediated – factors which enabled powerful actors to defend a liberally organized financial market environment: externally, international communication and bargaining processes have been and still are structurally biased towards a liberal global financial order owing to the strong role of global financial centres and the dynamics of competitive deregulation; and internally, the emergence of a new European economy, based on financial market integration and various processes of financialization, has brought about fundamental changes of European capitalism, as well as of societal and intergovernmental power relations. It is this context of half-hearted political compromises, of the incorporation of larger social strata into financialized European capitalism (Deutschmann 2011), and of a pertinacious European debt and banking crisis with its intimidating public effects that, to a considerable extent, forces in favour of liberal financial markets regained control over issues of global and European financial (re-)regulation.

In order to highlight how these aspects interplayed in averting European claims for a stronger and more comprehensive financial reform, the contribution is organized as follows: it starts with a short, theoretically guided outline of the politico-economic dynamics and organizational patterns which have been promoting the transition to finance-dominated accumulation over the past decades (Section 2). Then, in Section 3, it deals with the unfolding of the financial crisis in Europe and the main causes of the rather reserved policy stance of the EU. In principle, this policy stance can be seen as an expression of a modified, but successfully defended hegemonic role of transnational finance. At the same time, however, it is also the outcome of a couple of intense struggles over defining the nature of the ongoing crisis and the appropriate measures to overcome it. These struggles should be seen as a primarily European affair. Nevertheless, they also have a strong global imprint and repercussion. Even, if the prospects of bringing global finance under political control are currently rather gloomy, the interaction between European and global developments must be taken into account, if one tries to explore the remaining chances of alternative political strategies (Section 4).

2. EMERGENCE AND REPRODUCTION OF EUROPEAN FINANCIAL CAPITALISM

At the present time, there are quite a few scholars who maintain that the political economy of the European Union has passed through a transition towards a transnational financial capitalism (Becker and Jäger 2012; Lapavitsas *et al.* 2012). This kind of capitalism is not only based on a transnationally interwoven finance-dominated regime of accumulation; it also includes complex forms of political regulation. Moreover, the development and articulation of these two dimensions are shaped by competing alliances of social forces composed of business associations, academics, experts and journalists, trade unions, non-governmental organizations (NGOs) and social movements, national governments and other state agencies. This indicates that the dynamics of European financial capitalism are only partially caused by the expansive and intrusive nature of financial markets and their erratic fluctuations; they are also caused by numerous political initiatives aiming to transform the surrounding institutional and regulatory setting. It would be too simple to interpret these initiatives as the expression of the structural power of transnational financial firms alone, as inherited institutional conditions and the interests and views of other forces matter, too. And particularly after the outbreak of the crisis, it became evident that, given the countervailing activities of politicians, regulators, trade unions and social movements, the reproduction of European financial capitalism should be seen as a complex, i.e., a contradictory, politically contested and interactively embedded process (Mügge 2013). More systematically, it makes sense to differentiate between three dimensions or spheres of the interactive embeddedness of European finance: the social relations of (re-)production; the global financial order; and (trans-)national state civil society relations (Cox 1981).

The interactive embeddedness into the social relations of (re-)production refers to the fact that financial relations are both dependent on and constitutive for the ways people organize their particular forms of societal (re-)production, including the applied technologies, as well as the interplay between different social groups, public and private enterprises or companies and private households (Cox 1987: 17–34). Financial relations are dependent on these and other organizational patterns, as the social relations of (re-)production have to generate sufficient financial rents, dividends and savings to keep the provision of credit running. At the same time, financial relations are constitutive for production, as investments are to a substantial extent enabled by the provision of financial shares or credit. How this interaction between production and finance is organized varies between capitalist models; hence, also within the EU. As a consequence of the crisis of Fordism in the 1970s and the increased accumulation of financial assets (Roxburgh *et al.* 2011). past decades have been marked by a gradual convergence towards the Anglo-Saxon style of a capital market-based provision of finance (Grahl 2011). To list only a few tendencies, in continental Europe market capitalization of companies increased significantly owing to waves of mergers and acquisitions and the mania for speculative gains of many investors. In addition, there was an acceleration and boom in share trading and stock exchanges became de-mutualized. At the same time, non-financial firms, particularly transnational corporations (TNCs), directed their attention more and more to securities markets, i.e., towards the interests of shareholders and institutional investors. These and other tendencies – not to forget the capital-market-related reforms of the famous 'Lisbon Strategy', i.e., the privatization of pensions and public infrastructure – indicate that European financial market integration has brought about a remarkable thrust in the making of a 'new European economy'.

This thrust was, however, not only caused by changed social relations of (re-) production but also by a transformation of the interactive embeddedness of European finance into global economic governance. The organization of the world economy – like the social relations of (re-)production – should not be conceived as simply given but as the outcome and expression of historically specific configurations of social forces, i.e., of the interaction of material power relations, intersubjective meanings and competing visions and political projects. Obviously, the interactive embeddedness of European finance changed remarkably over past decades. Under the conditions of the Bretton Woods System (BWS) – fixed exchange rates in combination with co-operative intervention capacities and capital controls – it was politically controlled and mainly focussed on domestic developments (Helleiner 1994). Yet, after the collapse of the BWS, i.e., the move to flexible exchange rates in combination with processes of competitive deregulation spurred by regulatory arbitrage, the global financial order turned into the 'Dollar–Wall Street Regime' (DWSR) which, according to Peter Gowan (1999: 24), rests on two mutually reinforcing pillars: the United States (US) dollar as the world's leading currency, and Wall Street as the main global centre for financial transactions. These two pillars gave the US – partially mediated by international institutions and regimes such as the International Monetary Fund (IMF) and World Bank, the World Trade Organization (WTO), the Bank for International Settlements (BIS) and a whole range of standard setting bodies (Helleiner 2011) – not only the means to determine the rules of global finance, i.e., open capital markets, flexible exchange rates, and international currency competition; they also provided the opportunity 'to create capital through credit and not simply or primarily through the accumulation of resources' (Cafruny and Ryner 2007: 24) and to integrate global financial markets– hence, also the European ones – into the domestic capital circuit of the US (Seabrooke 2001).

Finally, state–civil-society relations represent the third sphere of the interactive embeddedness of European finance. State–civil-society relations focus on the specific forms and strategies by which socioeconomic and global issues are politically articulated in public discourses and state practices. In order to emphasize the mutual dependence and interpenetration of state and civil society one can – referring to the Gramscian concept of the 'extended' or 'integral' state – speak of a 'state-civil society-complex' (Cox 1981: 134) which includes both the political society and civil society. The political society is the state in a rather narrow sense, i.e., the ensemble of legislative, administrative and juridical institutions responsible for the definition and enforcement of collectively binding rules, regulations and decisions; while the civil society represents an institutionalized discourse arena. Mostly, it backs the authority of state apparatuses by generating a certain degree of public consensus, but sometimes it undermines given state authority as well. This also applies to the – nationally still fragmented – European state–civil-society complex which emerged over past decades. In the area of European finance, it has fostered a whole series of initiatives aiming to liberalize and to interactively embed financial markets via the creation of European legislation (directives and regulations) and the establishment of supranational state apparatuses such as the European Central Bank (ECB), a strengthened European Commission or of supra- and transgovernmental regulatory committees. At the same time, this institutionalization process was accompanied by increased political activities on the part of civil society organizations, primarily business associations (Bieling 2003; Mügge 2006).

The emergence of European financial capitalism and the related global political capacities of the EU must be placed in the outlined context of its threefold interactive embeddedness. At first glance, it seems as if all forms of this embeddedness have been mutually strengthened via European financial market integration. While the latter accelerated the modernization of given capitalist models, this modernization also buttressed the gradual development of a transnational – however, business-dominated – financial state–civil-society complex, which in turn increased the influence of the EU in different fora of global economic governance. In a way, such a stylized view of a direct relation between closer integration and external European power corresponds to the official self-perception of European actors. On closer inspection, however, the simplified and one-dimensional nature of such a view becomes visible. For, if one tries to explore the impact of capital-market-oriented integration on the social relations of (re-)production, it is difficult to overlook some profound socioeconomic contradictions and problems. They concern, for instance, the detrimental effects which short-term-oriented global finance generates for the more co-operative, trust-based and long-term-oriented continental capitalist models (Amable 2003; Cafruny and Ryner 2007: 43–71); and they concern in particular the fact that finance-dominated accumulation in combination with its specific forms of political organization – above all the monetarist bias and the asymmetrical governance of EMU, i.e., a centralized and binding monetary policy in combination with decentralized social and labour policies – has remarkably stimulated the uneven economic development across the EU, above all within the eurozone (Becker and Jäger 2012).

3. THE FINANCIAL CRISIS AND ITS IMPACT ON EUROPEAN (AND GLOBAL) FINANCIAL GOVERNANCE

While the mentioned problems were already given but lingering in the 1990s and 2000s, they became apparent with the outbreak of the global financial crisis. Even more, the financial crisis made evident that the chosen path of finance-dominated development was very risky, as it intensified European dependence on the US economy. Eventually, however, the course of the crisis and its political management took a strange turn. First, given the strong economic downturn, the collapse of share prices and interbank lending, the consequential rise of unemployment and social spending, European financial capitalism caused very high economic and social costs (Overbeek 2012: 38–40). Then, however, the public absorption of large parts of these costs and the emergence of a so-called 'sovereign debt crisis' became one of the core reasons why the interim ambitions to implement far-ranging and comprehensive financial re-regulation suffered defeat. The main reasons for this move can be found in the particular modes of sociopolitical interaction which contributed to the persistence of pre-crisis patterns of embeddedness. In this sense, the defeat of European ambitions can be interpreted as the combined effect of three – partially structural, partially relational – developments. The first, primarily structural development was the stepwise, although uneven and specific, incorporation of economic sectors, companies and social groups into the finance-dominated mode of capitalist accumulation within the EU. The second development consisted of the formation of influential political alliances in core action fields: while the governments of Germany and the so-called 'Nordic countries' plus the Commission averted the claims for more common resources by pushing through fiscal austerity, the (re-)regulation of financial markets was repelled by a transnational alliance under the leadership of the City of London and transnational financial capital; and besides, there have been important processes of alliance formation beyond the European area as well.

3.1. The impact of the global financial crisis in the EU

Before turning to the different areas of sociopolitical interaction, we have to assure ourselves of the material and discursive impact of the global financial crisis within the EU. Of course, the crisis had its origin in the US; and it was structurally caused by the mode of operation of the DWSR. This regime systematically generated financial bubbles to the extent that the Federal Reserve promoted an overrated US dollar and the treasury – via improving the attractiveness of Wall Street – stimulated financial capital inflows in order to balance a structural current account deficit. In this sense, the financial crisis has shown that, owing to unbalanced current accounts in combination with highly volatile capital flows, the global reproduction of financial capitalism is inherently instable and crisis-prone. Moreover, the stepwise integration of the European Economy into the DWSR and the orientation of European financial market integration on the US model have aggravated the crisis within the EU (Grahl 2011). It is by far no accident that particularly those economies have been fiercely hit by the crisis whose financial institutes were actively engaged in the US and whose models were characterized by a pronounced capital market orientation and comprehensive financialization. Besides, the economies to which this applies less have also been impaired by the crisis as a consequence of the global slump in the exports of goods and services. It would be, however, too one-sided to see the European course of the crisis only determined by global trade and capital flows. Also, the asymmetrical regulation of Economic and Monetary Union (EMU) and the unbalanced European division of labour strongly controlled by the West European export and surplus economies (Becker and Jäger 2012) contributed to the crisis as well. Imbalanced EU-internal current and capital accounts and the insufficient common political steering instruments (Aglietta 2012; Hall 2012) provide the very conditions which can be exploited by investment funds, hedge funds and other financial market players to launch profitable speculative attacks and to discipline potentially irresponsible national governments.

The vagaries and disciplinary impact of transnational financial markets generated the political mood that financial liberalization went too far depriving national governments of necessary political control and steering capacities. It was therefore no surprise that quite a few politicians questioned the priorities of the past and called for a comprehensive re-regulation of finance. If this call was not transposed into a corresponding political agenda, this can be ascribed to two structural features of European financial capitalism.

The first feature is the inclusion and submission of ever more areas of socio-economic reproduction to finance-dominated accumulation, i.e., the dynamics of financialization (Deutschmann 2011: 353–65; Crotty 2008). For instance, on a structural level there was a steep rise of the value of financial assets as a percentage of GDP in most economies, which reflects an increasing role of financial market players, particularly of the so-called FIRE sector (finance, insurance and real estate). This development brought about a transformation of social power relations affecting the mode of operation of the credit system, of corporate governance, and also of the state apparatuses. All these areas became more or less – directly or indirectly – exposed to international capital flows and the short-term moves of institutional investors. Yet, not only had these kinds of financial players gained in public influence, their activities are also based on a fairly comprehensive financialization of everyday life (Ertük *et al.* 2008). The latter process includes an increased indebtedness, but also more savings and greater reliance of private households on financial market developments, e.g., in the areas of housing, pensions or public infrastructure. Of course, this reliance generally also allows for regulatory measures working against the volatility of financial markets. At the same time, however, it restricts the coverage of all those efforts which are perceived as deleveraging disposable financial assets and undermining the financialized nature of the European economy.

While this first feature points towards more individualistic and potentially conservative attitudes of small and big holders of financial assets, as they certainly have something to lose during the crisis, the second feature shows that such fears are unevenly spread within the European Union (Lapavitsas *et al.* 2012). As a consequence, the financial crisis affected the national economies specifically (Becker and Jäger 2012; Bohle and Greskovits 2009). Immediately after the outbreak of the financial crisis, the 'fear of falling' was particularly pronounced in countries such as the United Kingdom (UK) and Ireland and, to a lesser extent, the Benelux countries, all characterized by an important and internationalized financial sector, widespread financialization and close relations with the US economy. Then, however, it also encroached upon the southern European countries – Spain, Portugal, Greece and partly also Italy – suffering from structural current account deficits and increased external indebtedness. It hit them to such an extent that their financial systems got to the brink of collapse and needed to be externally stabilized on the part of the creditor economies.[1] In turn, the creditors from the surplus economies, i.e., the transnational banks, savers and tax payers of Germany, Austria, the Netherlands and Scandinavian countries, suffered from the global financial crisis, too – but to a lesser extent. More importantly, they became increasingly concerned about secondary crisis effects caused by the public costs of economic stimulus programmes and bank rescues.

3.2. The management of the sovereign debt and euro crisis

European initiatives of crisis management must be interpreted against the outlined background of a transformed interactive embeddedness of finance into the social relations of (re-)production as well as into transnationalized, if, however, still intergovernmentally fragmented, state–civil-society relations. This was already evident in the first phase of crisis management when, confronted with collapsing banks and steeply declining share prices, governments – particularly those of the highly financialized economies – turned towards comprehensive banking bailout funds and economic stimulus programmes (Lapavitsas *et al.* 2012: 35–58; Pisani-Ferry and Sapir 2010: 353–9). Supported by an accommodating and pragmatic monetary policy of the ECB and other central banks, this move to stabilize the European economy was temporarily successful. However, in a mid-term perspective, it caused a steep rise of public indebtedness and increasing concerns of creditors as to whether their given credits will be served in the future. In order to prevent inflationary dangers and to reduce the risk of loan defaults, they partly re-nationalized their business strategies and became engaged for a policy change, i.e., a so-called 'exit strategy' which was mainly launched by the governments of surplus or creditor economies, transnational banks and the European Commission.

In view of the lingering euro crisis, the renewed retreat of public engagement remained, however, declarative and highly ambiguous. This means that international creditors and their political representatives – governments, inter- and supranational institutions, and transnational associations – agreed to establish common bailout funds for highly indebted states, i.e., the European Financial Stability Facility (EFSF) and the European Stability Mechanism (ESM), to stabilize the eurozone. At the same time, however, they made their financial support conditional on the implementation of a European agenda of austerity management. What this implied became particularly apparent in countries like Greece, Portugal and Ireland, which have been forced by the so-called troika composed of the IMF, the ECB and the European Commission to implement far-reaching austerity measures to improve their competitiveness by an 'internal devaluation' via reduced public expenses, shrinking social security provisions, postponed investments in public infrastructure and lower wages (Bieling 2012). Such measures are particularly pronounced in the most severely affected crisis countries, but by no means limited to them. On the contrary, since 2009 or 2010 almost all EU member states announced more or less radical austerity packages; and in addition, they agreed to make this orientation permanent through a series of crisis-constitutionalist[2] reform initiatives.

In spring 2010, a first initiative in that context was the introduction of a so-called 'European Semester' prescribing a new procedure which aims to establish an *ex-ante* co-ordination of national economic, financial, but also labour and social policies. A second crisis-constitutionalist initiative was the so-called 'Sixpack' – five regulations and one directive – which redefined the Stability and Growth Pact (SGP) in a stricter sense. The stricter rules concern the level of overall public indebtedness, macro-economic imbalances and the procedure of reversed qualified majority voting. Thirdly, the 'Euro Plus Pact', reflects a French–German compromise. Although the pact is not a generally binding EU arrangement but only a self-commitment of eurozone governments plus voluntary members, it further reinforces the competitiveness discourse on lower labour costs, more flexible labour markets, reduced social expenses, or convergent tax policies. More recently, the governments also agreed on a 'Fiscal Compact' and a Banking Union. The Fiscal Compact is legally problematic, as it is placed outside European treaty law but aims to modify it. In terms of content, it goes in the same direction as the Sixpack and even moves beyond it, since it binds the signatory states to codify European budgetary prescriptions in national constitutions or the like. The Banking Union represents rather a concession to hard suffering crisis economies. Prospectively, it should allow their banks to receive credit directly from the ESM, after a new banking supervision centralized at the ECB and a transnational deposit system are operational.

In view of the overall economic constellation and considerations to further stabilize EMU through common debt management and intensify economic co-ordination (European Council 2012), it is likely that crisis-constitutionalist initiatives will continue. The previous initiatives have been primarily supported and shaped by the private financial sector and its associations, think tanks and associated academics. Above all, transnational banks and their associations have been pushing to stabilize distressed states through the provision of common financial resources; either via the EFSF/ESM or via bond-buying programmes on the part of the ECB in order to ward off credit defaults. At the same time, as important organizations of the international creditor community, banks were also involved in the debates on stricter economic and budgetary rules (Corporate Europe Observatory [CEO] 2011).

3.3. Contested issues of financial re-regulation

While the crisis-constitutionalist initiatives have been strongly promoted by the governments and institutions of the creditor countries, above all by the ordo-liberally oriented German one, the constellation of political forces was different in the field of financial re-regulation. Of course, German politicians were also influential here. However, their liberal orientation has been softened owing to the destabilizing impact of unfettered financial markets. In other words, with respect to both the requirements of an economic model with a strong industrial base and ordo-liberal convictions, German actors agreed on a stricter legal, rule-based and stability-oriented re-regulation of European finance (Hall 2012: 367), while the governments and business associations from highly financialized economies, in the first line the British one, tried their very best to ward off or water down most re-regulation proposals. In general, the British policy stance reflects a preference for more informal, convention-based practices and the overwhelming centrality of the City of London for the British economic model. A few numbers may illustrate this: in 2010 financial services in the UK made up 10 per cent of GDP. The respective data for the US (7.5 per cent), Japan (6.7 per cent), France (4.6 per cent) and Germany (3.8 per cent) are significantly lower; and if one includes finance-related professional services (3.9 per cent of GDP), they are together more important than the manufacturing sector, which only contributes to 12 per cent of GDP in the UK (Talani 2011: 16).

Given this centrality, it was no surprise that the City of London and the British government, as well as most (transnational) financial firms and associations, have been on full alert and immediately became very active when the first proposals of financial re-regulation were put on the table. Obviously, the situation differed from pre-crisis times. Quite a few financial market issues, such as capital adequacy standards, a financial transaction tax (FTT), drying out of offshore financial centres (OFC), the regulation of hedge funds and rating agencies or the remuneration of management, were hotly debated in the public. Or, in the words of some colleagues:

> Before the crisis, financial regulation in the Union had been a classic zone of low politics: a domain dominated by dense networks inhabited by corporate elites and econocrats. After the crisis, competing visions of a reconstructed regulatory order and 'grandstanding' in defence of the interests of national markets became central to the high politics of the Union. (Engelen *et al.* 2011: 165)

It was the politicization of financial market issues which seduced some observers to see the EU already on its way to realize a fundamental change of the prevailing policy paradigm (Posner 2010); and although others have been more cautious, they also identified a turn towards a more market-shaping policy approach (Moschella 2011; Quaglia 2010). Conceptually, this turn corresponded with a discredited 'efficient market hypothesis' and an increasing influence of macroprudential thinking (Baker 2013). At least partly, this new mode of thinking was reflected in the proposal of the high-level expert group chaired by Jacques de Larosière (Larosière *et al.* 2009) to reorganize the European system of financial market supervision. From early 2011 onwards, three supranational supervisory authorities – the European Securities and Markets Authority (ESMA) in Paris, the European Banking Authority (EBA) in London and the European Insurance and Occupational Pensions Authority (EIOPA) in Frankfurt – started their work. They are complemented by a European Systemic Risk Board (ESRB), whose task is to identify potential financial instability risks as early as possible (Buckley and Howarth 2010: 124–9; Lannoo 2011; Semmler and Young 2010). Formally, these newly established authorities point to a further, but in the case of banking – therefore, the following initiative to establish a Banking Union – still insufficient centralization of European financial market control.

Apart from these reforms, it has become evident over the past years that structural conditions and power relations as well as manifold lobbying activities on the part of transnational finance have undermined the original impetus towards comprehensive re-regulation. In terms of the structural conditions, the dynamics of 'competitive deregulation', i.e., lowering of regulatory standards in face of transnational capital mobility, still represent a major barrier for establishing stronger political control of finance (Rixen 2013); even more so, as neither the economic nor the discursive power resources of transnational financial firms and their associations have been significantly diminished over the course of the crisis. Confronted with the heightened public salience of financial market issues, however, financial organizations had to adapt their lobbying activities. Before the crisis, they had been able to veto adverse regulatory proposals immediately at the very first stages of agenda-setting and policy formulation. In the meantime, as a consequence of the crisis, they resort to more subtle strategies which focussed on dilution and implied above all proposals of self-regulation and deferred implementation (Young 2013), but increasingly they also start to exploit regulatory arbitrage and engage in their traditional scaremongering activities again.

Therefore, and taking stock of hitherto steps of financial re-regulation, only modest results have been achieved (Buckley and Howarth 2010: 129–36; Quaglia 2012; Wahl 2010). Again and again, the European Commission submitted legislative proposals which were diluted and delayed after intense lobbying on the part of European finance. Consequently, for instance, rating agencies have to register and show how they generate their ratings and how they avoid conflict of interests. Simultaneously, however, pressures from the City of London secured that these rules have no impact on the activities of most influential US-based agencies such as Standard & Poor's, Moody's and Fitch. Or take the regulation of the so-called 'shadow banking systems' via a directive on Alternative Investment Funds Managers (AIFM), which applies to hedge funds, private equity funds or real estate funds: although in the future all these funds have to comply with the requirements of a European passport, such as an adequate risk and liquidity management, customer protection and supervision through ESMA, their very basic business models have not been questioned but only marginally modified. Furthermore, all those funds registered outside the EU, for instance in OFCs, got the concession of not becoming burdened with EU rules. And finally, the original agreement of the G20 summit in Pittsburgh in autumn 2009, which pretended to divert Over the Counter (OTC) trade in derivatives to official trading platforms, was also watered down in the implementation process. Instead of restricting this kind of trade, the European Market Infrastructure Regulation (EMIR) only requires that future derivative contracts must be registered and – in order to obviate payment default – cleared by regulated central counterparties.

The outlined developments indicate that despite all political efforts within the European multi-level system, financial firms and associations secured specific regulatory exceptions and loopholes. These loopholes do not only enable or facilitate the reproduction of the shadow banking system (Rixen 2013), they also exert a strong deregulatory pressure on the official credit system and traditional banking. This may apply less for the UK, where banks have been sufficiently capitalized owing to past rescue programmes and had the ability to mobilize – often overrated – risk-weighted assets (Howarth and Quaglia 2013). As compared to the UK, the financial conditions for many continental European banks are more strained and their respective national, European and global associations worked hard to water down the stricter regulatory proposals for the new Basel III accord. Negotiated within the Basel Committee on

Banking Supervision (BCBS) from July 2009 onwards, these proposals aimed to strengthen capital requirements (common equity and risk-weighted assets), to decrease bank leverage ratio and to promote countercyclical buffers. They were generally welcomed by all governments, although these proposals, particularly the calculation of risk-weighted assets, seemed to be inadequate to prevent further crises processes (Micossi 2013). These limitations notwithstanding, the transnational banking community, above all the Institute of International Finance (IIF), lobbied intensively to lower the new regulatory standards and give banks wider margins of discretion. Given the direct access of the IIF to the BCBS and the promotion of a public discourse on a too high burden and related risks for the world economy, the IIF has been successful in reducing core capital quota and deferring the transposition deadline to 2019 (Baker 2010; CEO 2012). In that context, it also received the backing of continental European governments ready to repel a regulatory enforced deleveraging of their banks (Howarth and Quaglia 2013).[3]

While the pre-conditions for stricter regulations in the area of banking have been generally favourable, the prospects for establishing a FTT on trading with shares, bonds and derivatives were clearly worse. Of course, for many social groups and political actors the argument that the financial sector has to share a certain proportion of the costs of the crisis, particularly in times of skyrocketing public debt, was compelling. At the same time, however, such a view was rejected by OFCs and highly financialized economies. Consequently, it turned out fairly soon that a FTT has no chance of being established on a global, but at best on a European, level. In September 2011, therefore, the European Commission (2011) made a first proposal which, however, owing to the requirement of unanimous decision-making in the field of taxation, met the effective resistance of some member states. In order to circumvent this resistance, the pro-FTT alliance of most governments, the European Parliament, parts of the Commission, trade unions and NGOs pushed for the application of the 'enhanced co-operation' procedure. After this has been accepted, the European Commission (2013) presented a second proposal which basically conforms with the first one – tax rates of 0.1 per cent for shares and bonds and 0.01 per cent for derivatives – but in addition to the 'residence principle' also suggests the application of an 'issuance principle', so that financial instruments of the FTT-zone would also be taxed elsewhere. This extension, in turn, has provoked protest and countervailing measures on the part of other governments and transnational finance (Wahl 2013). While the UK filed an action against the FTT, Goldman Sachs has launched a disputable report based on rather dubious numbers which do not take the cooling effect of the FTT into account; and the initiative to bring the ECB, with its expertise but close personal ties to transnational finance, into play further overshadows the prospects of the FTT (CEO 2013).

The outlined struggles over financial re-regulation reflect the particularities of each sectoral sphere and are shaped by the specific transnational constellation of business models, related interests of actors and inherited regulatory settings.

Compared to the pre-crisis period these particularities enabled a gradual extension and strengthening of regulatory standards. At the same time, there have been at least two factors which militated against too far-reaching expectations: first, the dynamics of 'competitive deregulation' impeded common European political control; and second, influential and active financial lobbying organizations (Engelen *et al.* 2011: 158–87; Haar *et al.* 2010) were alert on any market-shaping, not to mention market-correcting, ideas. Moreover, after the interim discursive defensive in 2008 and 2009, financial centres such as the City of London and the manifold organizations of transnational finance – for instance, the Institute of International Finance (IIF), the Alternative Investment Management Association (AIMA), the European Banking Federation (EBF) or the European Banking Group (EBG) – mobilized the competitiveness discourse again in order to highlight the dangers of a threatening over-regulation and over-burdening of financial services and a corresponding negative impact on the whole economy.

3.4. Actors and political alliances within and beyond the EU

The global debates and financial market initiatives run in parallel to the European ones. They deal with same or similar issues, however, in a slightly different and even less coherent institutional setting. In the past, the global setting emerged rather incrementally with the stepwise liberalization of financial markets. Consequently, from the mid-1970s onwards, the old Bretton Woods institutions – IMF and World Bank – were supplemented by a whole range of specific standard-setting bodies in the area of banking (1974), securities markets (1983), payments and settlements (1990), insurance (1994) and accounting (2001) (Helleiner 2011). In addition, the Asian financial crisis gave birth to a Financial Stability Forum (FSF) and the G20, composed of the former G7 and major emerging market economies, in 1999. Although the relevance and impact of the latter forums remained doubtful, both made a remarkable comeback with the outbreak of the global financial crisis. The FSF was re-established as the Financial Stability Board, while the G20 became the core arena for the global co-ordination of policy measures in the fight against the financial crisis.

Next to intensified communication between the various kinds of finance ministers, central bankers and governmental experts, there was a dense succession of G20 summits from autumn 2008 onwards: Washington (November 2008); London (April 2009); Pittsburgh (September 2009); Toronto (June 2010); Seoul (November 2010); Cannes (November 2011); Los Cabos (June 2012); and Moscow (September 2013). However, even a few years later, the effect and impact of all the activities initiated via the G20 are difficult to assess. In an attempt of interim stocktaking one may agree that, irrespective of some policy co-ordination and regulatory proposals, there has been only limited progress in bringing global finance under political control (Helleiner 2011; Soederberg 2012). At best, it is possible to identify an incremental – stability-oriented

– modification of a market-liberal order. In view of the heterogeneous membership of the G20, this outcome is not really surprising. However, if the different areas of activities are regarded separately, the situation is a bit more complex. In a way, the global developments mirror, by and large, the European ones; particularly, if one differentiates between three fields of action.

The first field refers to the co-ordination of most important emergency measures immediately after the outbreak of the crisis. They basically concerned monetary and exchange rate policies of central banks, the avoidance of protectionist instruments and the launch of economic stimulus programmes. In 2008 and 2009, co-ordination within the G20 was fairly intense in all these areas. Of course, it would be exaggerated to ascribe the relative stabilization of the global economy to the G20 alone. However, without it the danger of a relapse into protectionist strategies like in the 1930s would have been much more severe. Moreover, there is reason to assume that G20 talks exerted additional pressures on continental European governments to acquiesce into co-ordinated economic intervention and stimulus programmes, although this move did not last very long. Confronted with rising public debt, the EU – and, in this case, above all the German government – also used the G20 to buttress their changed political priorities in mid-2010. As noticed by an informed observer:

> Germany went into the G-20 meeting in Toronto on June 26–27 largely isolated. Before the meeting, President Obama publicly pleaded with Angela Merkel to change her policies. At the meeting the tables were turned. Canada's Stephen Harper as the host and David Cameron, the newly elected Conservative prime minister of the UK, lined up behind Merkel, leaving Obama isolated. Supporting Merkel's approach, the G-20 endorsed a halving of budget deficits by 2013 as the target. (Soros 2010)

Next to macro-economic management, the G20 focused on financial re-regulation. Not all, but many of those regulatory issues which were discussed, negotiated and implemented within the EU have also been dealt with by the G20 and the responsible sectoral standard-setting bodies such as the BCBS, the International Organization of Securities Commissions (IOSCO) or the International Accounting Standards Board (IASB) (Helleiner 2011). While the G20 mostly agreed on general aims, concrete reform suggestions have been contested; and via their delegation to international standard-setting bodies, financial groups and centres applied diverse lobbying techniques to dilute more ambitious proposals. Consequently, many regulatory loopholes and discretionary financial practices and also the much criticized shadow banking could be preserved (*cf.* Rixen 2013). This indicates that – perhaps with the exception of the Basel III accord – the watering down and deferral of regulatory reforms had a strong Anglo-American imprint. It concerned issues such as the winding down of systemically important financial institutions, the regulation of credit rating agencies and hedge funds, OTC markets and naked short-selling (Helleiner 2011).

Finally, from time to time, the G20 also deals with global current account imbalances and their potential attenuation through a co-ordinated exchange rate policy and capital controls. From the European side such issues are mainly promoted by the French government, while the more market liberal countries such as the US, the UK, but also Germany as a structural current account surplus country, are traditionally more sceptical or even hostile to the establishment of multilateral political steering capacities (Dullien 2012). In view of a significant veto power bloc, it is not surprising that little has happened in this field so far.[4] In other words, the EU remains rather hesitant to develop a more comprehensive and market-interventionist approach in order to counteract globally, as well as internally, the destabilizing current account imbalances.

These few remarks on core areas of financial market regulation show that the G20, even if its concrete impact remains difficult to assess, represents an important governance forum. It must be emphasized, however, that the G20 is only a forum, not an international organization. This means that it has no power of its own but depends on the engagement and compliance of participating actors. The network character of the G20 explains why European actors take it serious without feeling strong pressures to harmonize their respective political positions. On the contrary, sometimes the G20 is rather taken and seen as an additional lever to form coalitions which may be supportive of the respective preferences in European disputes. This applies above all to the UK which, in accordance with the US and the global financial services industries and their associations (Baker 2010), uses the G20 to strengthen its EU-internal bargaining position. Disregarding such specific tendencies, the main result is, however, that general political debates and alliances within and beyond the EU are rarely contradictory but mostly complementary.

4. CONCLUSION: THE EU AND GLOBAL FINANCIAL GOVERNANCE

This contribution asked why the more far-reaching ambitions of financial re-regulation which emerged after the outbreak of the global financial crisis were defeated. It was assumed that a more comprehensive answer can be found, if one explores the multi-faceted interactive embeddedness of European finance into the social relations of (re-)production, into the state-civil society relations and into global economic governance. Such a perspective shows that recent political developments are far from unambiguous. Instead, they are related to controversial and contradictory processes. Until the outbreak of the crisis, these processes have been marked by a gradual convergence towards an Anglo-American style of finance-dominated capitalist development. In the course of this convergence, the different dimensions of interactive embeddedness changed remarkably. Then, the crisis put the financial market policy approach of the European Union – which can be seen as an expression of this transformation – into question, while the impact of this questioning remained limited.

This indicates that the different modes of the interactive embeddedness of finance have changed to a certain extent but less so in term of the power relations inscribed to European financial capitalism. Obviously, the finance-dominated mode of accumulation and the manifold forms of financialization did persist. They have only been modified by new forms of state intervention and stability-oriented regulations. This is not to maintain that the financialization of European capitalism was a one-way street without any leeway for more far-reaching political reforms. Quite the contrary; past years have been marked by an overall politicization of finance and intense political and discursive struggles (Froud *et al.* 2012). In this way, the contribution tried to outline how these struggles evolved in the most important areas of European crisis management; and it arrived at the conclusion that more ambitious European reforms were diluted or deferred by area-specific – hegemonic – political alliances. For instance, a more solidaristic and growth-generating development, i.e., the very basis for a globally stronger European stance, was vetoed by Germany and other current account surplus countries, transnational creditors and tax payers. Slightly different was the constellation in the area of financial market (re-)regulation. Here, the UK and the City of London, together with the counter-lobbying on the part of transnational financial business associations, prevented a strategic reorientation transcending beyond the prevailing agenda of modest regulatory stabilization. A similar tendency can also be found in global financial governance, where the EU was neither able nor willing to push for more substantial measures in order to politically control globalized finance again.

In contrast to the tendency of attributing the latter aspect to the fragmented representation of the EU in global forums such as the G20, the emphasis in this contribution was on some other factors, above all the political articulation of EU-internal preferences. To avoid any misunderstanding: fragmented external representation may have a potentially constraining impact on European influence. However, in case of the current constellation, the very content of European – not only global – financial market policies indicates that the EU – or to be more precise, the European state–civil-society complex – is rather self-constraining and still in favour of a largely market-liberal approach. In doing this, the hegemonic European forces might benefit from supportive, i.e., similar or complementary processes in the US and within the G20. In this way, there is no one-sided relationship between the G20 and the EU. The interaction between both arenas should rather be interpreted and analysed as one between complementary systems of communicative channels.

Biographical note: Hans-Jürgen Bieling is professor of political economy at the Department for Political Science, Eberhard Karls University of Tübingen, Germany.

ACKNOWLEDGEMENTS

A first draft of this contribution was presented in a workshop on 'The EU in Global Finance' at the University of Amsterdam (UvA), 14–15 February 2013. For helpful comments and advice I would like to thank two anonymous referees, Tony Porter, Daniel Mügge, and the other participants of the workshop.

NOTES

1 Quite a few economies of Central and Eastern Europe have been confronted with similar sets of problems at an even earlier stage. However, as most of them lacked the advantage of being a member of European Monetary Union (EMU), they only disposed of weak levers to bail in European creditor countries.

2 Here, the term 'crisis constitutionalism' does not refer to constitutionalist changes in the strict sense of the word. Instead, it is derived from the political economic debate and the notion of 'new constitutionalism' invented by Stephen Gill (1998). In general 'new constitutionalism' addresses the broader changes of international treaties and the institutional and regulatory embeddedness of transnational capitalism. While it can be seen as the outcome of rather systemic and depoliticized tendencies of insulating the management of market-liberal globalization from democratic control, the term 'crisis constitutionalism' represents more controversial, ambiguous and therefore politicized changes of the transnational judicial and institutional setting.

3 In view of the still sluggish economic development and financial strain, it seems rather likely that banks will use the long implementation phase of Basel III for achieving even more flexible rules and procedures.

4 However, it is not precluded at all that things might change in the future when China and the US make concessions in terms of a more multilaterally orchestrated exchange rate regime.

REFERENCES

Aglietta, M. (2012) 'The European vortex', *New Left Review* 75: 15–36.

Amable, B. (2003) *The Diversity of Modern Capitalism*, Oxford: Oxford University Press.

Baker, A. (2010) 'Restraining regulatory capture? Anglo-America, crisis politics and trajectories of change in global financial governance', *International Affairs* 86(3): 647–63.

Baker, A. (2013) 'The gradual transformation? The incremental dynamics of macroprudential regulation', *Regulation & Governance* 7(4): 417–34.

Barber, L, Benoit, B. and Williamson, H. (2008) 'Regulation model has failed, says Merkel', *Financial Times*, 11 June.

Becker, J. and Jäger, J. (2012) 'Integration in crisis: a regulationist perspective on the interaction of European varieties of capitalism', *Competition & Change* 16(3): 169–87.

Bieling, H.-J. (2003) 'Social forces in the making of the new European economy: the case of financial market integration', *New Political Economy* 8(2): 203–24.

Bieling, H.-J. (2012) 'EU facing the crisis: social and employment policies in times of tight budgets', *Transfer* 18(3): 255–71.

Bohle, D. and Greskovits, B. (2009) 'East-Central Europe's quandary', *Journal of Democracy* 20(4): 50–63.
Buckley, J. and Howarth, D. (2010) 'Internal market: gesture politics? Explaining the EU's response to the financial crisis', *Journal of Common Market Studies* 48(Annual Review): 119–41.
Cafruny, A.W. and Ryner, M. (2007) *Europe at Bay. In the Shadow of US Hegemony*, Boulder, CO: Lynne Rienner.
Corporate Europe Observatory (CEO) (2011) 'Business against Europe. BusinessEurope celebrates social onslaught in Europe', available at http://corporateeurope.org/printpdf/348 (accessed 29 April 2013).
CEO (2012) 'Addicted to risk', available at http://corporateeurope.org/sites/default/files/publications/Addicted%20to%20risk.pdf (accessed 29 April 2013).
CEO (2013) 'Robbing the "Robin Hood" tax: the European Central Bank weighs in', available at http://corporateeurope.org/financial-lobby/2013/07/robbing-robin-hood-tax-european-central-bank-weighs (accessed 15 April 2013).
Cox, R.W. (1981) 'Social forces, states and world orders: beyond International Relations theory', *Millennium: Journal of International Studies* 10(2): 126–55.
Cox, R.W. (1987) *Production, Power, and World Order. Social Forces in the Making of History*, New York: Columbia University Press.
Crotty, J. (2008) 'If financial market competition is intense, why are financial firm profits so high? Reflections on the current "golden age" of finance', *Competition & Change* 12(2): 167–83.
Deutschmann, C. (2011) 'Limits to financialization. Sociological analyses of the financial crisis', *European Journal of Sociology* 52(3): 347–89.
Dullien, S. (2012) 'Anspruch und Wirklichkeit der Finanzmarktreform: Welche G20-Versprechen wurden umgesetzt?', *IMK-Study 26*, Düsseldorf: HBS.
Dür, A. and Elsig, M. (2011) 'Principals, agents, and the European Union's foreign economic policies', *Journal of European Public Policy* 18(3): 323–38.
Engelen, E. *et al.* (2011) *After the Great Complacence. Financial Crisis and the Politics of Reform*, Oxford: Oxford University Press.
Ertük, I., Froud, J., Johal, S., Leaver, A. and Williams, K. (2008) *Financialization at Work: Key Texts and Commentary*, London: Routledge.
European Commission (2011) 'Proposal for a Council Directive on a common system of financial transaction tax and amending Directive 2008/7/EC', COM(2011) 594 final, Brussels, 28 September.
European Commission (2013) 'Proposal for a Council Directive on implementing enhanced cooperation in the area of financial transaction tax', COM(2013) 71 final, Brussels, 14 February.
European Council (2012): 'Towards a genuine Economic and Monetary Union', Interim Report, Brussels, 12 December.
Froud, J., Nilksson, A., Moran, M. and Williams, K. (2012) 'Stories and interests in finance: agendas of governance before and after the financial crisis', *Governance* 25(1): 35–59.
Germain, R. (2009) 'Financial order and world politics: crisis, change and continuity', *International Affairs* 85(4): 669–87.
Gill, S. (1998) 'European governance and new constitutionalism: economic and monetary union and alternatives to disciplinary neoliberalism in Europe', *New Political Economy* 3(1): 5–26.
Gowan, P. (1999) *The Global Gamble. Washington's Faustian Bid for World Dominance*, London: Verso.
Grahl, J. (2011) 'The subordination of European finance', *Competition and Change* 15(1): 31–47.

Haar, K., Vassalos, Y. and Rowell, A. (2010) 'Banking on the bankers – regulation and the financial crisis', in Alter-EU (ed.), *Bursting the Brussels Bubble*, Brussels: Alter-EU, pp. 87–93.
Hall, P. (2012) 'The economics and politics of the euro crisis', *German Politics* 21(4): 355–71.
Hall, B., Barker, A. and Bryant, C. (2009) 'Sarkozy claims credit on tighter regulation', *Financial Times*, 2 April.
Helleiner, E. (1994) *States and the Reemergence of Global Finance: From Bretton Woods to the 1990s*, Ithaca, NY: Cornell University Press.
Helleiner, E. (2011) 'The limits of incrementalism: the G20, the FSB, and the international regulatory agenda', *Journal of Globalization and Development* 2(2): Article 11: 1–19.
Hervé, A. (2012): 'The participation of the European Union in global economic governance fora', *European Law Journal* 18(1): 143–61.
Howarth, D. and Quaglia, L. (2013) 'Banking on stability: the political economy of new capital requirements in the European Union', *European Integration* 35(3): 333–46.
Lannoo, K. (2011) 'The EU's response to the financial crisis – a mid-term review', *CEPS Policy Brief, No. 241*, Brussels: CEPS.
Lapavitsas, C. *et al.* (2012) *Crisis in the Eurozone*, London: Verso.
Larosière, J. de *et al.* (2009) 'Report from the High-Level Group on Supervision in the EU', 25 February, Brussels.
Micossi, S. (2013) 'A viable alternative to Basel III. Prudential capital rules', *CEPS Policy Brief, No. 291*, Brussels: CEPS.
Moschella, M. (2011) 'Searching for a fix for international financial markets: the European Union and domestic politico-economic changes', *Journal of Contemporary European Studies* 19(1): 97–112.
Mügge, D. (2006) 'Reordering the marketplace: competition politics in European finance', *Journal of Common Market Studies* 44(5): 991–1022.
Mügge, D. (2013) 'The political economy of Europeanized financial regulation', *Journal of European Public Policy* 20(3): 458–70.
Nesvetailova, A. and Palan, R. (2010) 'The end of liberal finance? Towards a changing paradigm of global financial governance', *Millennium: Journal of International Studies* 38(3): 797–825.
Overbeek, H. (2012) 'Sovereign debt crisis in euroland: root causes and implications for European integration', *The International Spectator* 47(1): 30–48.
Pisani-Ferry, J. and Sapir, A. (2010) 'Banking crisis management in the EU: an early assessment', *Economic Policy* 25(April): 341–73.
Posner, E. (2010) 'Is a European approach to financial regulation emerging from the crisis?', in E. Helleiner, S. Pagliari and H. Zimmermann (eds), *Global Finance in Crisis. The Politics of International Regulatory Change*, London: Routledge, pp. 108–20.
Quaglia, L. (2010) 'Completing the single market in financial services: the politics of competing advocacy coalitions', *Journal of European Public Policy* 17(7): 1007–22.
Quaglia, L. (2012) 'The regulatory response of the European Union: the case of hedge fund regulation' in R. Mayntz (ed.), *Crisis and Control. Institutional Changes in Financial Market Regulation*, Frankfurt a.M.: Campus, pp. 171–95.
Rixen, T. (2013) 'Why reregulation after the crisis is feeble: shadow banking, offshore financial centers, and jurisdictional competition', *Regulation & Governance* 7(4): 435–59.
Rommerskirchen, C. (2013) 'Keeping the agents leashed: the EU's external economic governance in the G20', *European Integration* 35(3): 347–60.

Roxburgh, C., Lund, S. and Piotrowski, J. (2011) *Mapping Global Capital Markets 2011*, San Francisco: McKinsey Global Institute.

Seabrooke, L. (2001) *US Power in International Finance. The Victory of Dividends*, Basingstoke: Palgrave.

Semmler, W. and Young, B. (2010) 'Lost in temptation of risk: financial market liberalization, financial market meltdown and regulatory reforms', *Comparative European Politics* 8(3): 327–53.

Smith, D. (2012) 'International financial regulation: a role for the eurozone?', *EU Diplomacy Paper 08/2012*, Brugge: College of Europe.

Soederberg, S. (2012) 'Class power, neoliberalism and the G20 summits', in R. Cox (ed.), *Corporate Power and Globalization in US Foreign Policy*, London: Routledge, pp. 162–84.

Soros, G. (2010) 'The crisis & the euro', *The New York Review of Books*, 19 August, available at http://www.nybooks.com/articles/archives/2010/aug/19/crisis-euro/?pagination=false (accessed 9 February 2014).

Talani, L.S. (2011) 'The impact of the global financial crisis on the City of London: towards the end of hegemony?', *Competition & Change* 15(1): 11–30.

Wahl, P. (2010) *Fighting Fire with Buckets. A Guide to European Regulation of Financial Markets*, Berlin: Weed.

Wahl, P. (2013) 'Massiver Angriff auf Finanztransaktionssteuer: Die Finanzlobby schlägt zurück', *Informationsbrief Weltwirtschaft & Entwicklung* July: 1–2.

Young, K. (2013) 'Financial industry groups' adaptation to the post-crisis regulatory environment: changing approaches to the policy cycle', *Regulation & Governance* 7(4): 460–80.

Zimmermann, H. (2010) 'Varieties of global financial governance? British and German approaches to financial market regulation', in E. Helleiner, S. Pagliari and H. Zimmermann (eds), *Global Finance in Crisis. The Politics of International Regulatory Change*, London: Routledge, pp. 121–36.

Losing abroad but winning at home: European financial industry groups in global financial governance since the crisis

Kevin Young

ABSTRACT This contribution examines the role of European Uion (EU) financial industry groups in global financial governance. I examine the extent to which EU-based financial industry groups are able to have their preferences met at different stages in the making of three different global banking regulatory policies which were part of the Basel III reforms. I find significant variation in their level of success – not across policies but across levels of governance. Specifically I find that the ability of these groups to affect either the global policy agenda or the specific content of new regulatory rules has been inconsistent and often quite weak, despite considerable structural power resources at their disposal and concerted advocacy campaigns. Where these groups have been more successful is in addressing the implementation phase, specifically EU-level implementation of these global regulatory policies. Such findings have implications not only for how we understand the power of EU financial industry groups in global governance generally, but also for more specific theoretical interventions on the role of market size, regulatory centralization and the structural power of firms.

1. INTRODUCTION

The issue of private sector groups within the financial industry, such as financial sector associations, individual firms and other networks of private authority, has been a major theme of inquiry both in the global governance literature and in research on European Union (EU) public policy specifically. This contribution examines the role of such EU-based financial industry groups in global financial governance. Through an examination of new global banking reforms, I examine the extent to which EU-based financial industry groups are able to have their preferences met at different stages in the policy-making process. I examine both the potential structural power advantages of EU banks as well as their organized lobbying campaigns, and find significant variation in their level of success – not across policies, but across levels of governance. EU financial industry groups have been largely unsuccessful 'abroad' but very successful 'at home'. The ability of these groups to affect either the global policy agenda or the specific content of new regulatory rules has been inconsistent and often quite weak. Yet, when it comes to the *translation* of these global regulatory policies into EU-level regulation, EU-based financial industry groups have been much more successful in their advocacy efforts, consistently gaining numerous exceptions and loopholes that meet their preferences.

These findings speak directly to existing literature and to the themes of this collection trying to ascertain the role of the EU in global financial governance. The evidence presented here suggests that recent arguments regarding the EU's market size and regulatory centralization as sources of the EU's financial power may be only conditionally true in the post-crisis period. Specifically, these and other kinds of power resources held by the EU as a bloc may relate to the regulatory autonomy of public authorities, but they don't necessarily extend to the ability of private authority to shape global regulatory rules in any extensive way. The active lobbying of EU financial industry groups does certainly play a role in global financial regulatory reform, but that role is quite circumscribed, with most major advocacy efforts losing more than they succeed when it come to the setting of global rules since the crisis.

The argument proceeds in four sections. In Section 2 I briefly describe extant literature in this area and argue that the design of global banking rules represent a 'most likely case' of EU financial industry influence over global regulatory outcomes. I set out the three different regulatory policies examined, each of which are part of the 'Basel III' Banking Accord, and argue that they exemplify different degrees of policy change in the post-crisis regulatory climate.

Section 3 assesses the extent to which EU-based financial industry groups had their preferences met at the very early stages of the policy-making process, based on an analysis of the distribution of costs imposed on EU banking systems compared to other jurisdictions. Section 4 details the advocacy efforts of EU-based financial industry groups over the content of these policies after they were first proposed. Section 5 details the results of these advocacy efforts, which suggest only minor instances where the design of global rules have been adapted in response to these efforts, but much more significant movement in the implementation plans for global rules within the EU in the form of the Capital Requirements Regulation (CRR).

Before proceeding, an important caveat is in order. It is important to emphasize that the analysis herein constitutes a descriptive-empirical argument, rather than an exercise in formal hypothesis testing in the vein of most interest group research. I do not seek to ascertain the particular conditions under which EU-based financial industry groups are successful in their advocacy aims or not. Doing so would require a different kind of research design than the one pursued here, and the focus of this contribution is on establishing the value of a dependent variable, not trying to explain the precise causes of that variation. In many studies of interest groups the policy outcomes are well known in advance (e.g., a policy favors this or that group, a new regulation gets watered down or strengthened, etc.). However, when it comes to the broad characterizations of 'who gets what' in global financial governance, the winners, losers and all those in-between are less immediately clear from the outset. This contribution attempts to shed some light on this area.

2. FINANCIAL INDUSTRY GROUPS AND EU POWER IN GLOBAL FINANCIAL GOVERNANCE

How do we make sense of the role of the EU in global financial governance? Much extant scholarship on global financial governance has pointed to the critical role of market size in conditioning financial power on the global stage (e.g., Braithwaite and Drahos 1999: 113; Drezner 2007: 23, 121; Simmons 2001), and this has traditionally pointed scholars toward the United States (US). The sheer size of US markets, and the structural importance of US financial markets in the global economy more broadly, has lent itself to the longstanding assumption that US regulatory institutions and, in turn, their local interest constituencies like the US-based banking and securities firms have held sway. Recent scholarship has challenged such a notion and pointed to the relative rise of Europe in global financial governance. Bach and Newman (2007) advance an argument that market size alone is insufficient as a determinant of regulatory influence on the global stage, pointing to the importance of powerful and capable regulatory institutions to affect the global agenda. On similar grounds, Posner (2009) has argued that the balance of financial regulatory power has been recast: the growing centralization of regulatory functions within EU institutions has reshaped the distribution of financial power across the Atlantic.

Global financial governance is understood to be multilevel in character (Helleiner and Pagliari 2011), and regulatory decision-making within Europe is now widely understood to have important global effects, as this collection underlines. In recognition of this, a substantial literature has developed to track and trace EU financial regulatory policy change since the crisis (Howarth and Quaglia 2013; Pagliari 2012; Quaglia 2012; Woll 2013). Most existing scholarship with a focus on the EU tends to focus on national-level lobbying directed at the course of EU-level policies (Macartney 2009; Woll 2013), at broad transformations in financial regulatory change within the EU over time (Busch 2008; Mügge 2009; Nölke and Perry 2006; Zimmerman 2010) or at exploring the interstate politics of how different intra-EU institutional environments react to global rules (e.g. Howarth and Quaglia 2013). While latent in some existing analyses, the role of EU financial industry groups in affecting *global* regulatory policies has not been a focus (exceptions include Fioretos [2010] and Kudrna [2013]).

How would one begin to assess the importance of EU-based financial industry groups in 'global' financial governance? In global financial governance the dominant mode of regulatory policy-making is the use of international financial standards (Gibbon *et al.* 2011), and while these are not the only means of global governance in this area they are often used as an indicator of which actors are exercising power (see Tsingou 2008; Underhill and Zhang 2008;

Young 2012). Within the banking sector, the primary transnational regulatory body designing these international standards it the Basel Committee on Banking Supervision (BCBS) – a transnational forum of banking regulators from 27 countries. The BCBS was charged with the design of new global banking rules in the form of 'Basel III' – so named because it is the third in a series of international regulatory packages, first in 1988 and second in 2004. Basel III is a good empirical focus for assessing the role of EU-based financial industry groups because it represents a 'most likely case' of financial industry influence over global regulatory outcomes.

There are three reasons why we might expect EU financial industry groups to get many of their preferences met in global rules. First, the EU is the most over-represented jurisdiction within the BCBS, since 10 of the 27 jurisdictions represented within the BCBS are EU member states. EU-based financial industry groups thus have more potential entry-points to have their preferences represented than other jurisdictions, since the decision-making rule is deliberative consensus.[1] Second, existing literature (mentioned above) also suggests that the EU's regulatory centralization should work in its favor. Not only has the EU been a loyal servant of international financial standards, but it has been particularly loyal when it comes to BCBS-based standards – for example the Capital Requirements Directive (CRD) has traditionally translated earlier Basel Accords more or less directly into EU legislation. This notably stands in contrast to jurisdictions like the US and Japan, whose implementation of international financial standards before the crisis has been lackluster at best.[2] Third, banks in the EU also possess a number of structural power advantages that should, according to some existing theory that I detail below, serve them well in terms of having their preferences met.

Basel III is considered emblematic of the kind of global reform processes under way since the crisis (see Helleiner 2012; Howarth and Quaglia 2013). It is also useful for another reason. As a complex international standard it is fundamentally a 'package' of many different regulatory policies within it. This allows us to select policies which are representative of a range of important regulatory changes that have taken place since the crisis. Most existing accounts of post-crisis financial regulatory change represent new regulatory policy output as a mixed bag: new policy approaches represent a mixture of policy continuity from the past with some important breaks from it; policies vary as well in the extent of their stringency. How would we select such a range of policies? Hall (1993) set out a useful metric for how to assess the particular extent of policy change, and recently scholars of financial regulation have begun to use this metric as a way to calibrate their own comparisons of post-crisis financial regulatory change (e.g., Baker 2013b; Carstensen 2011; Hodson and Mabbett 2009). Essentially policy is broken down into three components: the policy instruments themselves; the settings of these instruments; and the hierarchy of goals underlying the policy. First-order policy change involves changes to the particular settings of the basic instruments of a policy, while the overall goals and instruments themselves remain the same. What Hall (1993) called second-order policy change referred to a situation where the policy instruments themselves (i.e., not just their settings) changed, even if the basic goals changed. Third-order change is associated with a more radical policy disjuncture, in that it represents a change in all three components of policy: instrument settings; the instruments themselves; and the hierarchy of goals behind policy (see Hall 1993: 278–9).

Table 1 summarizes the policies chosen for analysis from Basel III. They vary not only in content but in the extent to which they represent different kinds of revisions to the existing global banking regulatory framework. The first of these is the new regulatory policy designed to increase the quality and the size of banks' capital adequacy buffers by increasing their high-quality 'Tier 1′ regulatory capital. The Tier 1 capital policy is thus representative of the effort to increase the particular 'settings' of instruments like risk-weighted capital adequacy requirements, after the widespread recognition of policy and market failure in the midst of the crisis. As such, it represents a 'first order' policy change, as indicated in Table 1.

The second regulatory policy examined, the 'leverage ratio', is a policy which represents more of a 'second order' change. This policy sets a limit on the amount of leverage that banks can have. Specifically, a banks' the ratio of capital to gross exposure cannot be greater than 3 per cent, meaning that a bank cannot lend more than 33 times their own capital. This represents a significant break from regulatory policies pursued since the late 1990s, since it is fundamentally a 'risk-insensitive' regulatory requirement. The third regulatory policy examined represents a more comprehensive or radical departure from earlier forms of bank regulation, and is not concerned with banks' capital at all, but with the management of their liquidity. According to Hall's (1993) criterion specified above, it represents not only a change in the instruments of policy but also in the hierarchy of goals. The 'Liquidity Coverage Ratio' (LCR) represents a form of policy learning from the Lehman Brothers crash in particular, when the banking system as a whole did not have a sufficient stock of liquid assets, causing a chain reaction of market illiquidity and uncertainty during September and October 2008 in particular. The thinking behind the LCR is related to the rise of fundamental paradigmatic shifts in thinking such as 'macroprudentialism', which existing scholarship takes to represent a third-order policy change (see Baker 2013a). The LCR is considered to be a macroprudential tool (see Van den End and Kruidhof 2013), and the macroprudential shift has been argued by previous literature to be a third-order policy change (Baker 2013b: 5).

3. ANALYSIS OF PRIVATE SECTOR INFLUENCE OVER THE EARLY AGENDA OF GLOBAL RULES

A rich tradition in the study of interest groups is the role of business in shaping the initial early content of rules, even before much of the (more readily 'traceable') lobbying takes place. This is especially important when considering the role of organized business. Financial industry groups might be considered yet

Table 1 Different regulatory policies under analysis and the characteristics of post-crisis financial regulatory policy thinking that they represent

Regulatory policy under analysis	*Meaning in post-crisis financial regulatory environment*	*Hall (1993) criteria of policy change*			*Concrete policy objectives*
		Instrument levels	*Policy instruments*	*Policy goals*	
1. Tier 1 capital increase	Increase in overall stringency	X			Increase the size and quality of banks' 'Tier 1' (highest quality) capital adequacy buffers
2. Leverage ratio	Departure from old models of regulation such as risk-sensitivity	X	X		Introduce a minimum level of banks leverage to act as a backstop/failsafe to limit bank risk
3. Liquidity Coverage Ratio	Use of macroprudentialism, shifted focus on liquidity-based risks within the banking system	X	X	X	Generate a new set of regulations to ensure the banking system can maintain sufficient liquidity during times of stress

more structurally privileged, because of the particular centrality of financial accumulation in the current phase of capitalist development. As highlighted above the existing literature on global financial power points to the role of market size and to regulatory centralization as key determinants of the EU's bargaining power. 'Market power' might be interpreted in multiple ways, but as Table 2 illustrates, by a variety of measures the EU holds a sizable share of most quantities plausibly of interest to the designers of global banking rules.[3] Not only the number of banks but also the value of total banking assets within the EU is higher than in other major jurisdictions like the US or Japan. When taking either the percentage of bank assets or bank capital held by BCBS countries in the 'Global Top 50' (a league table of the largest banks in the world [*The Banker* 2012]), banks in the EU also have a greater share than other jurisdictions. As Table 2 illustrates, each of these comparisons hold even when the UK is removed from the count.

While the structural importance of banking varies across EU member states, when considering the EU as a whole banking is a more fundamentally important source of commercial financing than other forms, such as equity financing (which is much more important in the US, for example). While this is for the most part a qualitative, institutional point, its manifestations can be measured quantitatively. Rows 5–8 of Table 2 illustrate numerous other ways in which one might measure the structural importance of banks and bank credit to an economy. Whether by the importance of banks deposits, loans by banks or credit, the EU features a more important role for of banking than other powerful jurisdictions such as Japan and the US.

Table 2 Structural characteristics of select banking systems

		EU-27	*USA*	*Japan*	*UK*	*EU-26*
1	Number of banks	7,162	6,291	142	368	6,794
2	Total assets of all banks (€ trillion)	35.9	9.8	8.3	8.1	27.8
3	Deposit banks assets to GDP (%)	118	64	187	192	115
4	Bank assets in the Global Top 50 (%)	45.3	15.2	11.2	14.5	24.0
5	Bank capital in the Global Top 50 (%)	36.9	22.9	10.2	12.9	30.8
6	Bank deposits to GDP (%)	175	59	132	221	–
7	Bank loans to GDP (%)	194	67	92	239	–
8	Private credit by banks to GDP (%)	140	55	106	192	137

Notes: All data corresponds to fiscal year-end 2011. EU-26 is all EU members minus the figures for the UK. Source data for rows 1–2 is EBFed (2011, Table 2). Source data for row 3 is from Čihák *et al.* (2012), and excludes data from Liechtenstein due to lack of available data. Source data for rows 4–5 is *The Banker Top 50* league table (*The Banker* 2012), with all calculations made by the author. Source data for rows 6–7 is EBFed (2011, Table 2). Source data for row 8 is from Čihák *et al.* (2012) and excludes data from Bulgaria, Czech Republic, Hungary, Liechtenstein, Latvia, Poland and Sweden owing to lack of available data. All calculated percentages rounded up to the first decimal place.

Taking the structural importance-as-power argument seriously entails the expectation that the content of global financial regulatory rules should favor EU financial industry groups in relation to other major jurisdictions such as the US. While different interpretations exist, structural power is usually understood to manifest itself most vividly in the initial phases of policy-making: at the stage at which the agenda is first set, and policies are either just being formed. This would correspond to the very early stages of Basel III's development – namely in the initial negotiation positions of regulators within the BCBS and more concretely manifest in the very first Basel III draft document, released in January 2009.[4]

How did EU-based financial industry groups fare in these early stages? The Tier 1 capital policy meant that banks around the world had to increase their levels of high-quality Tier 1 capital. This meant a significant increase in regulatory costs, whether banks had their home jurisdictions in Tokyo, Toronto, New York, Paris or Frankfurt. However, European banks were (and still are) much less well capitalized in terms of high-quality Tier 1 capital than their US counterparts, for example, making the policy more costly in relative terms for the EU. Some of the details of what banks could actually include as Tier 1 capital also represented a disadvantage. One particular detail of the policy was to severely restrict the use of hybrid securities – financial instruments that were treated as both debt and equity. Traditionally hybrid securities had been used most extensively in Japan; however, the use of hybrid securities was on the rise exactly when Basel III was first being designed. Between July 2008 and July 2009, European banks raised approximately $30 billion in hybrid securities to recapitalize, and the figure was expected to grow.[5] European banks from various national jurisdictions, among them Standard Chartered (UK), Credit Agricole (France), Deutsche Bank (Germany) and Société Générale (France), had all made significant hybrid security issuances in 2009 (see Alexander 2008; *Euroweek* 2009). The introduction of a policy which directly penalizes these financial instruments thus speaks to the inability of EU-based financial industry groups to inform the policy agenda in line with their preferences.

Yet, while the EU was hit hard by the Tier 1 capital policy, there is some evidence that their structural importance may have played a role in ameliorating an *even worse* result. Jurisdictions that had particularly severe banking crises, namely regulators from the United States (in particular the Federal Deposit Insurance Corporation [FDIC]), the United Kingdom and Switzerland all strongly favored an increase in Tier 1 capital to 9 per cent of risk-weighted assets. Regulators from France and Germany, however, objected to such a sharp increase, and the policy was set instead at 6 per cent, allowing for national discretion to impose higher standards if they liked (Walker [2011], confirmed in interview 10 July 2011, Berlin). This suggests a potentially significant structural role for European banks, whose preferences may have been channeled through their regulators during this stage in the policy-making process. While this helped moderate the severity of costs for them, the costs were still substantial – French banks, for example, calculated a €360 billion deficit in Tier 1 capital, a 40 per cent shortfall.

The leverage ratio policy represents a more straightforward instance where EU banks faced significant costs relative to other jurisdictions. The ratio, set at 3 per cent (thus constraining banks' leverage to be no greater than 33 times their equity), was actually modeled after US banking regulation,[6] and has been a longstanding tool for US regulators (principally the Federal Deposit Insurance Corporation) to limit bank leverage on deposit-insured banks. While US banks already faced leverage ratios, no such risk-insensitive 'backstop' on bank leverage was ever in place in EU banking regulation.[7] Not only is the policy 'foreign' to their regulatory environment, but the leverage of many European banks was often significantly higher than in other jurisdictions at the time in which the policy was conceived. The mean leverage of *all* French banks for which data were available in 2008 was 34.2; for Austria mean leverage was 50.9, and for Finland it was 58.3 (see Kalemi-Ozcan *et al.* 2012: 296). The firm-level story is more instructive: large and structurally significant banks like Deutsche Bank, Barclays, Royal Bank of Scotland, and BNP Paribas had leverage of 49.7, 49.0, 43.3, 39.7 and 35.2, respectively. During the same period, large US investment banks like Bear Stearns, Merrill Lynch and Lehman Brothers had famously high leverage (of 33.5, 33.4 and 30.7 respectively) – yet none of these institutions persisted into the next year, as Merrill was absorbed into Bank of America and, the other two famously went to the wall.

The Liquidity Coverage Ratio (LCR) policy was also much more costly in relative terms for EU-based banks than in other major jurisdictions. Like the other policies described above, the LCR policy represented a new cost for banks everywhere, the US included; however, for European banks the policy represented a truly substantial adjustment. The LCR requires banks to have a stock of high quality liquid assets on hand at any given time to withstand a 30-day period of extreme financial distress. As initially proposed, European banks would have had to raise an additional 2 trillion euros in highly liquid assets and 3.5–5.5 trillion euros in long-term funding to comply with the LCR, with the majority of these funds concentrated in the largest 16 European banks (Härle *et al.* 2010: 4). Nearly two-thirds of the global liquidity shortfall was located in Europe (Slater 2013).

For each of these regulatory policies there were significant costs shouldered by EU-based banks. To be sure, not every bank in Europe would suffer the exact same consequences of these policies – regulatory policy-making has very firm-specific redistributive effects. But as far as broad generalizations are concerned, the general pattern is relatively clear: as initially proposed, these three Basel III policies left banks in the EU faring less well than their counterparts in other major jurisdictions. The Tier 1 capital policy was least costly to EU groups, and the leverage ratio and LCR much more costly, but taken together there is good evidence *against* the proposition that EU-based financial industry groups exercised effective influence over global financial regulatory rules at the agenda-setting phase of regulatory policy-making.

4. FINANCIAL INDUSTRY ADVOCACY OVER THE DETAILED CONTENT OF GLOBAL RULES

When it comes to the detailed, often highly technical, content of financial regulatory rules, there is often a process of *revision* to regulatory policy content after it is first laid out. While the structural conditions emphasized above are important in this context, the focus here is on the kinds of arguments EU-based financial industry groups made, and the ways in which they mobilized in an attempt to induce desired changes to regulatory policy content. In what follows I describe some of the advocacy activities surrounding each of the policies under analysis, and in each case document which of these were successful and which were not, at both the 'global' BCBS level in the form of the Basel III agreement and the 'local' EU level through the Capital Requirements Regulation (CRR).

4.1. Advocacy over the Tier 1 capital policy

EU-based financial industry groups engaged in advocacy around the Tier 1 capital policy, but not in the way that one might first expect. Efforts were not, on the whole, directed toward the overall raising of capital *per se* (the policy instrument itself), but rather against the particular details of the policy or, in Hall's (1993) terms, the setting of the instruments' levels. National regulators in many EU member states had already signaled their willingness to raise capital requirements in their own national jurisdiction, which made fighting the global regulatory standard a less 'winnable' option.[8] There was also recognition among some EU-based groups that the politicization of banks' capital would make a concerted campaign difficult, given the high salience of the issue (Culpepper 2011), and the related fact that the BCBS was given a strong mandate from the G20 leaders to increase the quality and quantity of bank capital.[9] Thus, rather than going after raising the capital base *per se*, EU groups launched three different kinds of advocacy campaigns.[10]

First, there was widespread advocacy for the restrictions of hybrid securities to be eased up. Specifically, a wide variety of EU groups advocated for the inclusion of certain 'innovative' hybrid securities into the capital base (BBA-GFMA-ISDA 2010: 11; Deutsche Bank 2010: 12; FBF 2010: 13–14). Second, EU groups went after the restrictiveness of the Tier 1 capital policy by going after the various criteria that Basel III stated banks had to *deduct* from their Tier 1 capital. Among these were goodwill, intangibles, investments in other financial institutions, deferred tax assets, mortgage servicing rights, excess expected losses, defined pension fund assets and the minority interests of banks. EU financial industry groups lobbied over a wide variety of these deductions, typically arguing that they should not be deducted from Tier 1 capital, but rather should be included into it.

Third, there was a widespread argument made to regulators regarding the *timing* of raising the Tier 1 capital base. Groups such as the European

Banking Federation (EBFed) and the European Financial Services Roundtable (EFSR) argued that, if implemented too soon, capital increases would damage the fragile economic recovery (EBFed 2010: 2; EFSR 2011). At high level meetings with BCBS members in June 2010, for example, this was one of the key demands of groups like the Association for Financial Markets in Europe (AFME), and subsequent follow-up with regulators maintained and reiterated these 'economy wide' concerns with implementation and timing. Financial industry arguments regarding the need to delay implementation have been used frequently since the crisis, not only in Europe but also by transnational groups (BBA-GFMA-ISDA 2010; IIF 2010) and by peak business associations such as *BusinessEurope* (2010: 2).[11] While the call for Basel III to be 'phased-in' over a period of time was a near universal position of private sector groups commenting on the issue across the globe, according to some accounts it was more positively received by EU regulators (Kudrna 2013: 197), possibly for the structural reasons described in Table 2.

4.2. Lobbying over the leverage ratio

Whereas EU financial industry groups articulated a fairly nuanced and detailed position with respect to Tier 1 capital, they argued more crudely and forcefully against the leverage ratio. It was argued to be an 'overly simplistic, non-risk sensitive tool ... [that] would constitute a huge step backwards' (EFSR 2010: 5–6), and 'a crude measure which contradicts the spirit and the purpose of the Basel II rules which take into account the riskiness of investments' (EBFed 2010: 6). Peak national associations in France and Germany argued a similar case, with the latter stating that it 'rejects the concept of the leverage ratio' (FBF 2010: 2, 7; ZKA 2010: 10). This position was extremely widespread in the EU, and reflects the relative cost disadvantage to EU banks, as emphasized above. The policy was not, notably, treated the same way by US financial industry groups – banks there quarreled with some of the technical content of the policy, but not the policy *per se* (e.g. see American Bankers' Association 2010: 2).

EU groups advocated having the leverage ratio removed as a binding constraint. The BCBS sought to 'migrate' the leverage ratio policy from Pillar II of the Accord (where it was essentially a matter of supervisory review) to Pillar I of the Accord (where it represented a binding regulatory constraint – see BCBS [2009a: 60]). A central plank of EU-based financial industry groups was to prevent such migration to Pillar I, and thus to make the policy non-binding. EU groups argued the case that national accounting systems made Pillar II more appropriate (EFSR 2010: 7–8), and many challenged the logic of the ratio (some nicknamed it 'Basel Minus 1" in discussions with regulators), frequently arguing that financial institutions in Europe have high leverage but no defaults.

When the BCBS conducted its own study of the leverage ratio's impact, the AFME countered its findings with more recent data (see AFME 2011). Individual banks from across the major economies of Europe argued strongly against the policy, disputing its usefulness on a wide variety of grounds (e.g., Barclays 2010: 4; BNP Paribas 2010: 2; Deutsche Bank 2010: 17). There was an understanding that, given strong US demand for the leverage ratio, even more intense lobbying would have to take place at the EU level. Here, too, EU financial industry groups were highly strategic in who they targeted. There were many meetings with Members of the European Parliament (MEPs), but because they felt there was considerable stigma within the European Parliament, they used their networks in different countries to get their issues raised with national regulators.[12]

4.3. Lobbying over the Liquidity Coverage Ratio (LCR)

The lobbying campaigns associated with the LCR policy were more focused and vociferous than for the other policies mentioned above. The financial industry across key jurisdictions such as France, Germany, Denmark and the UK, as well as pan-EU associations, made concerted efforts to convince the BCBS to include a wider range of financial instruments as part of banks' liquidity coverage. Two different kinds of lobbying campaigns ensued.

The first was designed to push for the inclusion of securitized financial instruments as part of banks' liquidity coverage. Specifically, beginning in 2010 the EFSR and the AFME partnered in a new initiative to *create* a brand new securitization certification system. Known as Prime Collateralized Securities, these new financial instruments are designed to grant a special label to higher quality asset-backed securities as well as increase their transparency (Duarte 2011). The explicit aim of this project was not simply to increase market confidence, but to gain regulatory approval for inclusion into the LCR (Connaghan 2012; interview, Brussels, 1 July 2013). The initiative had the support of members of the European Central Bank and the European Investment Bank from the beginning, eventually securing senior officials from both institutions to their Board (PCS 2012).

The second kind of lobbying campaign which emerged in reaction to the LCR had to do with a very specific kind of financial instrument called 'covered bonds'. Covered bonds are debt securities which, like many asset-backed securities (ABS), are backed by cash flows associated with mortgages or public sector loans. One of the reasons why the LCR policy was so punitive to European banks was because, in the first draft of the new Basel III Accord, the BCBS proposed a 50 per cent limit on the use of covered bonds as part of banks' liquidity coverage (BCBS 2009b: 9). Furthermore, these financial instruments were subject to a 20–40 per cent haircut, depending on their credit rating (BCBS 2009b: 10–11). Covered bonds are a very small percentage of the global total – 2.4–2.8 per cent of total eligible highly liquid assets, according to the BCBS's monitoring reports (BCBS 2012a: 20, 2012b: 26). Covered bond markets are enormously significant for financial markets and the mortgage systems in countries such as Germany and Denmark in particular, and banks in these jurisdictions were particularly active and vociferous in their advocacy

(Watt 2011; interview 8 July 2011, Berlin; interview, Brussels, 5 November 2013; Jenkins and Hughes 2010; Schwartzkopff 2012), and specialized groups within the mortgage industry (such as the European Covered Bond Council within the European Mortgage Federation, for example) endeavored to subsidize national campaigns with pan-EU data to back up technical points (interviews 14 June 2011, 4 November 2013, Brussels).

5. REVISIONS TO GLOBAL AND EU RULES

This section details the series of changes and non-changes that were made to the three policies under analysis, focusing on both formal revisions made to Basel III and to the EU 'translation' of Basel III in the form of CRD IV, the formal transposition of Basel III into EU regulations. CRD IV is made up of both the Capital Requirements Directive (CRD), which is implemented through national law, and the Capital Requirements Regulation (CRR) which is made applicable to all banks across the EU. The three policies under analysis fall under the CRR. Table 3 outlines the different changes made at the Basel and EU levels for the policies examined and the specific advocacy campaigns highlighted above.

5.1. Changes to Tier 1 capital policy

Of the three concerted campaigns of EU financial industry groups, there was mixed success. The restriction of hybrid securities was not eased, but a number of deductions listed above were changed. There were some small but significant changes made to the allowance of minority interests and banks' investments in other financial institutions, both up to certain restricted limits (see BCBS 2010a: 1–2). Deductions for deferred tax assets were also softened, but only for those which resulted in changes in timing, and mortgage servicing rights could be included, but only up to 10 per cent of a banks' capital base. These small exemptions could have provided more significant cumulative capital relief if it weren't for the fact that the BCBS limited the total amount that these instruments could be counted, up to a maximum of 15 per cent of capital *combined*, which is quite limited. Much more significant was that subsequent revisions to Basel III announced that the total Tier 1 capital that banks would be phased in over several years, first moderately from 2013 until 2019, when the full policy would be fully in place.

It is difficult to assess to what extent EU financial industry groups specifically contributed to the changes that took place, especially given that many of the changes advocated (especially the timing concern) were part of a global chorus. Indeed, while EU financial industry groups made strong cases for the need to 'phase-in' new global reforms, so did financial industry groups and other actors in nearly every jurisdiction. What is more clear is the fact that the extent of policy change in financial industry groups' desired direction was much more extensive when it came to the EU implementation of Basel III

Table 3 Regulatory policies under analysis, their associated lobbying campaigns in the EU, and varying levels of success

			Advocacy success	
Name of Basel III regulatory policy	*Costs imposed by policy as first proposed*	*Lobbying campaigns by EU groups*	*'Global' level: Basel III document*	*'Local' level: capital requirements regulation (CRR)*
1. Tier 1 capital policy	Moderate – ameliorated by Germany, France and Japan	Hybrid securities Deductions Timing of policy	None Some minor changes Phasing-in of implementation	Exclusions made Significant changes Grandfathering of capital instruments by 10 years
2. Leverage ratio	High	Move to pillar II (non-binding)	None	Flexibility in timeline; future process to revisit the need for the policy by 2015; exemptions made for SMES.
3. Liquidity Coverage Ratio (LCR)	Very high	Promotion of prime collateralized securities Covered bonds	No change, though phasing-in of implementation overall Some very minor changes	Considerable flexibility in what instruments can be included in the LCR

regulations, the Capital Requirements Regulation (CRR). Hybrid capital instruments, while not changed in Basel III from the first draft to the final, received special treatment in the EU, where they are allowed, albeit in a restricted way, and must be written down when Common Equity Tier 1 capital falls below 5.125 per cent. Also in contrast to Basel III, the CRR also has even more extensive recognition of minority interests, and it allows for significant investments in unconsolidated financial entities, whereas Basel III restricted these. Specifically, it allows for the consolidation of banking and insurance entities in a group. These changes to EU-level implementation of Basel III are, notably, much more extensive in their revisions than the US implementation of Basel III, which have mainly made exemptions for mortgage servicing rights.

5.2. Changes to the leverage ratio

Despite the efforts detailed above, the design of the leverage ratio within Basel III did not change, and no provision was made to stop a migration to Pillar 1 (see BCBS 2010b). Neither the structural importance of banking in the EU, nor the higher leverage of many large EU banks relative to large US banks appear to have affected the regulatory outcomes. UK banks knew extremely well that the Bank of England and the Financial Services Authority (FSA) was strongly in favor of the policy, and peak-EU associations learned very quickly in their engagements with Brussels that the leverage ratio was 'politically decided'. When national banking associations in France and Germany communicated their concerns to their respective national regulators, they learned that there was little disagreement, that their regulators were supportive, but that there was no real room to move in light of the positions held within the rest of the BCBS.[13] Thus, while EU-based groups may have succeeded in gaining the support of some regulators, they did not succeed in getting their regulators to successfully bargain for their preferences within the BCBS.

Yet, within the EU, in the CRR the leverage ratio policy has also been adjusted in a way more in line with financial industry preferences. While previously the Commission was enthusiastic to translate new global financial regulatory rules into EU regulations, now the Commission has stated that 'it is important to gather more information before making the leverage ratio a binding requirement' (see European Commission 2013: 5). The Capital Requirements Regulation stipulates that EU institutions will conduct their own monitoring period and evaluation, departing from the global one set out by the BCBS. Specifically, the European Banking Authority is mandating that banks report their leverage ratios to it starting in 2015, and will report to the European Commission by the end of October 2016 whether 3 per cent leverage is an appropriate level. The Commission has also announced that it will apply lower conversion factors (parameters within the leverage ratio policy for off-balance sheet items) for some financial instruments connected to trade finance and lending to small businesses in Europe. To be sure, these changes do not constitute an unequivocal advocacy victory, as there is still uncertainty with respect to the future; however, the door has been opened wider to new opportunities for advocacy in the future.

5.3. Changes to the LCR

There were a series of small changes to the LCR within Basel III, and these came in incremental stages. Most were only marginally in line with the demands of EU financial industry groups. At the second draft of Basel III, the LCR was noticeably eased slightly in terms of the restrictions on the use of covered bonds. The 50 per cent limit for the use of covered bonds as highly liquid assets was changed to 40 per cent, and the 20–40 per cent haircut on the value of covered bonds was changed to a flat 15 per cent, and other restrictive criteria, such as the need to use 10 years of historic data to have covered bonds eligible for inclusion, were dropped (see BCBS 2010a: 9–10). These changes were not, however, interpreted as a significant advocacy victory by the main industry groups fighting for this change (interviews 4 and 5 November 2013, Brussels).

After sub-committee meetings on the LCR in September and December 2012, the BCBS agreed to a list of further changes to the LCR, which were announced in January 2013. The major change was simple: a much more gradual phasing in of implementation. Now only 60 per cent of the LCR minimum is required beginning in 2015, 70 per cent in 2016, etc., until the LCR level reaches 100 per cent in 2019. As for the covered bonds issue, the January 2013 document did not bring the long sought-after regulatory changes that EU interest groups had advocated for. The EU-based attempt to get the BCBS to include Prime Collateralized Securities (PCS) into the LCR failed (Leask 2013). Instead, the BCBS expanded the allowances for Residential Mortgage Backed Securities (RMBS) – specifically RMBS' that are subject to 'full recourse', meaning the borrower is fully liable for the loan, even if the property value fails below the loans' value. This model is much more common in Europe than in the US (*Euroweek* 2013; Hintze 2013), suggesting it may be a concession to the EU as a whole, but there is no evidence that this was a change that was specifically advocated for, and groups active on this policy did not interpret it as significant (interviews 4–5 November 2013, Brussels).

Within the EU translation of Basel III the door is left open for the inclusion of other asset classes into the LCR. Specifically, the Commission has indicated the potential for flexibility in implementation with the LCR, and has announced that it *will not* fix the list of liquid assets that banks can use (which Basel III does), instead leaving this to research within the European Banking Authority (EBA). In his regard the EBA is to have regard for the Basel III definition, but to take EU and national specificities into account. Other changes were made which represented further lenient treatment. For example, CRD IV makes adjustments to the LCR in terms of how corporate payments for trade finance transactions are accounted for. Under Basel III, banks are only able to assume that 50 per cent of their corporate exposures were actually going to come due in the next 30 days – a relatively conservative assumption. Under the CRR, banks can assume that 100 per cent would come due. The CRR also empowers the EBA to count liquid assets at the group level, rather than at the individual bank level as Basel III prescribes.

6. CONCLUSION

This contribution has examined the role of EU-based financial industry groups in global financial governance. I have examined three key policies which represent different degrees of regulatory policy change since the financial crisis: policies regarding bank capital; leverage; and liquidity. For each, I have examined the extent to which EU-based financial industry groups were able to have their preferences met at different phases of the policy-making process.

I first examined the early formation of these policies when they were put on the global regulatory policy agenda. While in one case some EU regulators managed to successfully moderate the stringency of a policy (Tier 1 capital levels), in general EU financial industry groups shouldered a proportionally higher cost than other jurisdictions such as the US. The analysis then moved to the organized advocacy efforts of EU financial industry groups, examining a variety of detailed policy changes that these groups sought on each of the three policies examined. Despite multifarious kinds of advocacy deployed, EU financial industry groups' success in helping bring about their desired policy changes was mixed. Some policy details of Basel III did move in their desired direction, but usually only modestly. Others simply did not budge. Interestingly, most of the changes that took place were often owing to the *timing* of new global banking rules, through a gradual 'phase-in' approach. These changes were significant by any standard, but given that private sector demands for such 'phase-in' were nearly universal, it may be the case that EU groups contributed to a global conversation, but didn't move global rules by their own accord.

These and other precise causal relationships in the advocacy process might be best explored in future research through focused and detailed process tracing. Yet what is nevertheless still clear is a disjuncture between global rules and local EU ones, in this case the transposition of Basel III into the EU Capital Requirements Regulation. In nearly every instance EU financial industry groups were more successful 'at home' in the transposition of global rules into EU regulations than 'abroad'. Indeed, as we have seen, many of the changes that they were sought in global rules that failed were acquired later, in EU-level policy-making. Yet, even when it comes to EU-level rules, it must be noted that policy changes are no clear 'slam-dunk' case of advocacy victory. European institutions have clearly generated a complex compromise between partly addressing financial industry concerns and still retaining discretion into the future. The pattern of 'losing abroad but winning at home' also suggest that EU-based financial industry groups have encouraged greater regulatory divergence from the US and elsewhere by bending the implementation process to local conditions, and in so doing may have exacerbated a situation of 'cooperative decentralization' (Helleiner and Pagliari 2011) that some now understood to be the new basis of global financial governance.

EU financial industry groups may be a force to be reckoned with within the EU, but on the global stage their preferences were rarely accommodated. These results are consistent with the findings of Kudrna (2013), who finds a lack of capacity and willingness for EU actors to project their power internationally during the same period, within both banking and accounting. However, these results are also inconsistent with the expectation that the structural importance of banks, either understood through market size or through their embeddedness in European economic institutions, allows private sector groups to affect global rules. The global regulation of banking is one area where EU financial industry groups might be expected to have considerable advantages – both in terms of international bargaining leverage and in terms of the structural power of firms to have their preferences represented and met. Consequently, their inability to structure the global agenda, even despite these advantages, either forces us to call into question their power or tells us that the EU members of the Basel Committee are less amiable to financial industry influence in global forums than they and others are within the EU-level policy-making process.

Biographical note: Kevin Young is an Assistant Professor in the Department of Political Science at the University of Massachusetts Amherst.

ACKNOWLEDGEMENTS

I thank the participants at the EU-GR:EEN Workshop, 'The European Union in Global Financial Governance', as well as many helpful comments from the 'Continuity and Change in European Finance and Its Governance' panel at the 2013 Council for European Studies International Conference of Europeanists. My grateful thanks go to the anonymous reviewers for their insightful critiques, and to Elliot Posner, Daniel Mügge and Stefano Pagliari for their helpful feedback on earlier drafts.

NOTES

1 While it is not always necessarily case that these member states speak with one single voice, a number of European institutions, such as the European Commission, the European Banking Authority and the European Central Bank, are all observer members of the BCBS, enhancing that possibility though their ability to monitor the negotiations. Mügge (2011) argues that EU power in international finance can be delimited when there is representation of both member states and EU institutions. However, in the case of the BCBS, it is member states that clearly have the

upper hand – they are the only formally 'voting' members with the full range of authority that this provides.

2 A key reason, it might be noted, for the US's non-implementation was its regulatory fragmentation: the Federal Reserve and the Treasury could not see eye to eye with the FDIC (see Bair 2012). For an account of uneven implementation patterns of Basel-based standards in Japan, see Chey (2006).

3 Table 2 includes additional data on the UK alone, since the US and UK are sometimes seen as allies opposed to 'Continental' EU preferences, and so that the figures for the EU and the US can be compared without the UK included.

4 Interviews conducted with a wide range of industry groups in the US, UK, Germany, France, Netherlands, and including EU-level groups, corroborated a story that their knowledge of the particular content of Basel III prior to December 2009 was either fully unknown or extremely fuzzy.

5 See data from Barclays reported in Piggott (2009).

6 Canada also had a leverage ratio policy in place in its national regulatory regime, but no other BCBS members did at the time.

7 Notably, however, the leverage ratio does include some add-ons for banks' off-balance sheet risks. Some US regulators such as the FDIC argued forcefully during the policy's construction for a much higher ratio, but were not able to achieve this (see Bair 2012: 264–5; Onaran 2012).

8 For example, during the design phase of this policy at the Basel level, national regulators in the UK, France, Germany, Italy, the Netherlands, Belgium and Switzerland had all signaled that regulatory capital would be increased in their national jurisdictions.

9 Interviews, 10 May 2011, London; 14 June 2011, Brussels.

10 As Culpepper (2011) points out, high salience politics doesn't necessarily mean that influence won't occur, but only that the tools relied upon earlier may not be as effective and groups will have to diversify their strategies.

11 Accounts by financial industry representatives themselves suggest that this was an issue with which industry voices and ideas had greater legitimacy. Interviews with EU financial industry group,s London 15 Jul 2011; Berlin 1 and 7 July 2011.

12 Interviews, Brussels 1 and 2 July 2013.

13 Interviews, 11 July 2011, Berlin; 27 August 2012, Paris.

REFERENCES

Alexander, P. (2008) 'Hybrid capital under scrutiny', *The Banker*, 1 August.

American Bankers' Association (2010) *Letter to BCBS Secretariat*, Washington, DC, 14 April.

Association for Financial Markets in Europe (AFME) (2009) 'Basel 3 and CRD 4', Press Release, London, 29 November.

Bach, D. and Newman, A. (2007) 'The European regulatory state and global public policy: micro-institutions, macro-influence', *Journal of European Public Policy* 14(6): 827–46.

Bair, S. 2012. *Bull by the Horns*, New York: Free Press.

Baker, A. (2013a) 'The new political economy of the macroprudential ideational shift', *New Political Economy* 18(1): 112–39.

Baker, A. (2013b) 'The gradual transformation? The incremental dynamics of macroprudential regulation', *Regulation and Governance* 7(4): 417–34.

Basel Committee on Banking Supervision (BCBS) (2009a) *Consultative Document: Strengthening the Resilience of the Banking Sector*, Basel: BCBS.

Banker, The (2012) Top 1000 World Banks 2012, 2 July, available at http://www.thebanker.com/Top-1000-World-Banks/Top-1000-World-Banks-2012?ct=true (accessed February 2014).
Barclays (2010) *Letter to BCBS Secretariat*, London, 16 April.
BCBS (2009b) *Consultative Document: International Framework for Liquidity Risk Measurement, Standards and Monitoring*, Basel: BCBS.
BCBS (2010a) *Annex to Changes Agreed*, Basel: BCBS.
BCBS (2010b) *Basel III: A Global Regulatory Framework for More Resilient Banks and Banking Systems*, Basel: BCBS.
BCBS (2012a) *Results of the Basel III Monitoring Exercise as of 30 June 2011*, April, Basel: BCBS.
BCBS (2012b) *Results of the Basel III Monitoring Exercise as of 31 December 2011*, September, Basel: BCBs.
BNP Paribas (2010) *Letter to BCBS Secretariat*, Paris, 16 April.
British Banking Association, Global Financial Markets Association, and International Swaps and Derivatives Association (BBA-GFMA-ISDA) (2010) *Letter to BCBS Secretariat*, London, 16 April.
Braithwaite, J. and Drahos, P. (1999) *Global Business Regulation*, Cambridge: Cambridge University Press.
BusinessEurope (2010) *Letter to BCBS Secretariat*, Brussels, 16 April.
Busch, A. (2008) *Banking Regulation and Globalization*, Oxford: Oxford University Press.
Carstensen, M.B. (2011) 'Ideas are not as stable as political scientists want them to be: a theory of incremental ideational change', *Political Studies* 59(3): 596–615.
Chey, H.-K. (2006) 'Explaining cosmetic compliance with international regulatory regimes: the implementation of the Basle Accord in Japan, 1998–2003', *New Political Economy* 11(2): 271–89.
Čihák, M., Demirgüç-Kunt, A., Feyen, E. and Levine, R. (2012) 'Benchmarking financial development around the world', *World Bank Policy Research Working Paper, No. 6175*, Washington, DC: World Bank.
Connaghan, C. (2012) 'Reviving a stigmatized market', *Wall Street Journal*, 20 June.
Culpepper, Pepper. (2011) *Quiet Politics and Business Power: Corporate Control in Europe and Japan*, Cambridge: Cambridge University Press.
Deutsche Bank (2010) *Letter to BCBS Secretariat*, London, 16 April.
Drezner, D. (2007) *All Politics is Global: Explaining International Regulatory Regimes*, Princeton, NJ: Princeton University Press.
Duarte, E. (2011) 'Asset-backed bond issuers plan quality label to lure buyers', *Bloomberg*, 28 September.
EFSR (2010) *Letter to BCBS Secretariat*, Brussels, 14 April.
EFSR (2011) *Letter to François Baroin*, Brussels, 17 October.
European Banking Federation (EBFed) (2010) 'Finding the right balance of the new basel framework', *Policy Paper*, 16 April, Brussels: European Banking Federation.
European Banking Federation (EBFed) (2011) *International Comparison of Banking Sectors*, Brussels: EBFed.
European Commission (2013) *European Banking Committee (EBC) Info-Letter 6*, September, Brussels: European Commission.
European Financial Services Roundtable (EFSR) (2011a) 'Letter to Jean-Claude Trichet', Brussels, 18 February.
Euroweek (2009) 'Hybridsleave bitter after-taste', 11 September, p. 66.
Euroweek (2013) 'ABS bankers call for more after Basel shift', 15 January.
Fioretos, O. (2010) 'Capitalist diversity and the international regulation of hedge funds', *Review of International Political Economy* 17(4): 696–723.

French Banking Federation (FBF) (2010) *Letter to BCBS Secretariat*, Paris, 16 April.
Gibbon, P., Ponte, S. and Vestergaard, J. (eds) (2011) *Governing Through Standards: Origins, Drivers and Limitations* (London: Palgrave).
Hall, P. (1993) 'Policy paradigms, social learning, and the state: the case of economic policymaking in Britain', *Comparative Political Studies* 25(3): 275–96.
Härle, P., Heuser, M., Pfetsch, S. and Poppensieker, T. (2010) 'Basel III: what the draft proposals might mean for European banking', Report, McKinsey, April.
Helleiner, E. (2012) 'The Limits of incrementalism: the G20, FSB and the international regulatory agenda', *Journal of Globalization and Development* 2(2): 1–19.
Helleiner, E. and Pagliari, S. (2011) 'The end of an era in international financial regulation? A post-crisis research agenda', *International Organization* 65(1): 169–200.
Hintze, J. (2013) 'Basel goes easy on RMBS, at least for European banks', *Asset Securitization Report*, 8 Feb.
Hodson, D. and Mabbett, D. (2009) 'UK economic policy and the global financial crisis: paradigm lost?', *Journal of Common Market Studies* 47(5): 1041–61.
Howarth, D. and Quaglia, L. (2013) 'Banking on stability: the political economy of new capital requirements in the European Union', *Journal of European Integration* 35(3): 333–46.
IIF (2010) 'Letter to Basel Committee on Banking Supervision',. Washington, DC, 16 April.
Jenkins, P. and Hughes, J. (2010) 'Danish banks urge changes to Basel III', *Financial Times*, 6 July.
Kalemli-Ozcan, S., Sorensen, B. and Yesiltas, S. (2012) 'Leverage across firms, banks, and countries', *Journal of International Economics* 88(2): 284–98.
Kudrna, Z. (2013) 'EU Financial market regulation: protecting distinctive policy preferences', in G. Falkner and P. Müller (eds), *EU Policies in a Global Perspective: Shaping or Taking International Regimes?* London: Routledge, pp. 186–204.
Leask, H. (2013) 'Only UK, Dutch RMBS may pass liquidity buffers hurdle', *Total Securitization*, 7 Jan.
Macartney, H. (2009) 'Variegated Neo-Liberalism: transnationally oriented fractions of capital in EU financial integration', *Review of International Studies* 35: 451–80.
Mügge, D. (2009) *Widen the Market Narrow the Competition*, Colchester: ECPR Press.
Mügge, D. (2011) 'The European presence in global financial governance: a principal–agent perspective', *Journal of European Public Policy* 18(3): 383–402.
Nölke, A. and Perry, J. (2006) 'The political economy of international accounting standards', *Review of International Political Economy* 13(4): 559–86.
Onaran, Y. (2012) 'US banks' leverage should be halved to cut risks, Bair says', *Bloomberg*, 26 September.
Pagliari, S. (2012) 'Who governs finance? The shifting public–private divide in the regulation of derivatives, rating agencies and hedge funds', *European Law Journal* 18(1): 44–61.
PCS (2012) 'PCS securitization label opens for business with senior board appointments', *Press Release*, 14 November.
Piggott, C. (2009) 'The capital conundrum', *The Banker*, 1 December.
Posner, E. (2009) 'Making rules for global finance: transatlantic regulatory cooperation at the turn of the millennium', *International Organization* 63: 665–99.
Quaglia, L. (2012) 'The "old" and the "new" politics of financial services regulation in the European Union', *New Political Economy* 17(4): 665–82.
Schwartzkopff, F. (2012) 'Denmark tells banks to ignore Basel on mortgage bonds', *Bloomberg*, 6 Dec.
Simmons, B.A. (2001) 'The international politics of harmonization: the case of capital market regulation', *International Organization* 55(3): 589–620.

Slater, S. (2013) 'Softer liquidity rules lift Europe's banks', *Reuters*, 7 January.
Tsingou, E. (2008) 'Transnational private governance and the Basel process: banking regulation and supervision, private interests and Basel II', in J.-C. Graz and A. Nölke (eds), *Transnational Private Governance and its Limits*, London: Routledge and ECPR, pp. 58–68.
Underhill, G.R.D. and Zhang, X. (2008) 'Setting the rules: private power, political underpinnings, and legitimacy in global monetary and financial governance', *International Affairs* 84(3): 535–54.
Van den End, J.-W. and Kruidhof, M. (2013) 'Modeling the liquidity ratio as a macroprudential instrument', *Journal of Banking Regulation* 14(2): 91–106.
Walker, G.A. (2011) 'Basel III market and regulatory compromis', *Journal of Banking Regulation* 12(2): 95–99.
Watt, M. (2011) 'Danish regulators push for more flexible Basel III liquidity rules', *Risk*, 3 Feb.
Woll, C. (2013) 'Lobbying under pressure: the effect of salience on European Union hedge fund regulation', *Journal of Common Market Studies* 51(3): 555–72.
Young, K. (2012) 'Transnational regulatory capture? An empirical examination of transnational lobbying over the Basel Committee on banking supervision', *Review of International Political Economy* 19(4): 663–88.
Zimmerman, H. (2010) 'Varieties of global financial governance? British and German approaches to financial market regulation', in E. Helleiner, S. Pagliari and H. Zimmerman (eds), *Global Finance in Crisis: The Politics of International Regulatory Change*, London: Routledge, pp. 121–36.
ZKA (2010) *Letter to BCBS Secretariat*, Berlin, 16 April.

Distinctions, affiliations, and professional knowledge in financial reform expert groups

Leonard Seabrooke and Eleni Tsingou

ABSTRACT Who determines what ideas matter in reform debates? This contribution examines reform proposals from the expert groups that emerged during the recent international financial crisis. To do so it follows fractal distinctions – distinctions that replicate themselves in subsequent iterations – among the reports. Fractal distinctions, such as between 'behaviour' or 'system' as a reform focus, allow us to locate the object of regulation within expert groups, the experts' professional context and the politics behind the commissioning of work. Analysing fractal distinctions provides a useful way to understand the different stresses in reports with and without clear mandates, and the role of important members of the policy community in promoting particular reform ideas. The contribution finds that differences in ideas emerging from the financial reform expert groups reflect nested power relationships in the commissioning of work, constituent audiences and reform priorities among governing institutions, rather than distinct 'European' and 'American' ideas.

INTRODUCTION

The international financial crisis of 2007–2009 generated strong demand for ideas on how to reform financial systems to become more stable and less prone to systemic paralysis. With demand firmly established, a range of intergovernmental organizations, private interest groups, and others provided ensembles to develop policy solutions for an eager transnational policy community, politicians, and public. Accordingly, the formation of what we refer to as 'financial reform expert groups' occurred quickly, with established transnational policy community members chosen to guide the development of reform proposals. By late 2009, 11 significant reports from such groups had been released. The reports had important differences in how the international financial system should be reformed, with some calling for 'plumbing' solutions within national systems while retaining the broader established international architecture, and others directly questioning the value of the financial sector to society and demanding system-wide reforms. For those chairing and working in the groups, there were institutional incentives to be on message with regard to the body funding the work and its perceived constituency. There were also professional incentives to provide a distinct contribution to the debate that would clarify and strengthen the signal to the policy audience during a period of 'noise'. Professionally, those working in expert groups had an interest in emboldening or maintaining their place and credibility in the transnational policy community. Ideas about reform shifted between how to regulate behaviour within the system and what should be done about the banking and financial system as a whole. During this period the banking system was identified as a 'threat to the sovereign' that could collapse the entire economy, a phrase associated with Iceland and Ireland.[1] This systems-level idea was soon replaced by discussions of 'too big to fail' that focused on very large banks as units to be regulated. Later, the designation of 'systemically important financial institutions' linked the behaviour and structure ideas, but with little clarity on what this meant for practical policy implementation. Similar dynamics could be found with macroprudential regulation as a broad idea from which policies would be developed. Debates over macroprudential regulation represented a 'gestalt flip' in thinking, but one that occurred without a paradigm shift from an established policy setting (Baker 2013). The obvious reason why is the trouble of accommodating structure-level thinking alongside political and welfare pressures in different financial systems. A further reason was that consensus was inhibited by professional desires for differentiation in policy recommendations.

This contribution deals with the distinctions made by different financial reform expert groups. Our concern is to assess why groups differed according to the policy proposals, the professional context for the work, and the politics behind the commissioning of the work. Proposals are distinguished from financial reform expert groups that emerged in 2008–2009, according to the combination of 'behaviour' and 'structure' thinking. We argue that the distinction between behaviour and structure is what Andrew Abbott (2001: 10–15) refers to as a 'fractal distinction', one that replicates itself in further debates about how to treat financial reform. From the first cut, groups debating financial reform will differ on whether they see the object of regulation as behaviour or structure. But from there, those who choose to focus on behaviour may well bring back in arguments about the need to regulate the structure, while those who are more single-minded will repeat the need to focus more intensely on behaviour. Financial reform expert groups operated with self-replicating distinctions, and those distinctions reflect not only different thinking about financial reform, but also professional logics and institutional incentives that are linked to the funding of the work and the group members' political constituency.

The contribution also outlines the affiliation network of key members of the expert groups to demonstrate the thick relational context in which these groups conducted their work. There is considerable traffic for particular individuals between meeting rooms for expert work. This is not surprising given the necessary level of economic and technical knowledge. Further, we suggest that on financial reform it is more important to understand actions from the transnational policy community in their professional and political contexts, rather than searching for distinctly 'European' or 'American' ideas for financial governance. This is in contrast to scholarly work suggesting that, post-crisis, the key question is which national or regional ideas about financial governance would dominate, including a distinctive European agenda (*cf.* Helleiner *et al.* 2009; Quaglia 2014).

Methodologically, the contribution relies on applying fractal distinctions from a document analysis of the 2008–2009 reports, as well as dozens of interviews with members of the transnational policy community, including several named authors of the studied reports. We consider 2008 and 2009 to be particularly important for financial reform reports, especially because the determination of what metrics to use, and key concepts and principles espoused, were arrived at in a 'hot' rather than 'cold' form of knowledge production, with various interest groups and organizations seeking to throw their weight around (Callon 1998). Several reports have been published since, but we find that key ideas were produced in that early period, and reports thereafter have mostly expanded and/or developed those ideas. As one G30 report participant commented in 2010, the 'window of opportunity for reform is already closed – reforms are now mostly driven by the international process'. In contrast, economists seeking to innovate in financial regulation expressed the view that the time span for reform was 10 to 15 years.[2] Our view is that even though the horizons for political actions and economic reforms differ, the early reports mattered both for those seeking to manage the crisis in the hot period, as well as for those seeking to transform ideas into actual policy in the cold long run. In addition to the document analysis and interviews, we draw upon experience while being actively engaged in the policy community of interest, primarily as a director and a commissioner of the Warwick Commission on International Financial Reform (2009), which was active from late 2008 to mid-2010.[3]

This contribution proceeds as follows. First, we outline fractal distinctions as a useful tool for understanding conflicts in a community that replicate themselves over time. Second, we detail how the financial reform expert groups of 2008–2009 differed in their emphasis on behaviour vs structure ideas for reform, taking care to provide detail on how exactly the reports varied in their policy recommendations, as well as what obvious silences can be identified. In particular, we show that the reports are more usefully differentiated along behaviour and structure lines and not the geographical origin of ideas. We note, in fact, that the only distinctive national/regional element among the reports is an emphasis on a speedy possible implementation in the European (De Larosière) exercise, which is lacking in the other examples. Third, we provide an affiliation network of key players in financial reform expert groups to show how this is a close-knit community. Finally, we bring together the analysis of fractal distinctions and the affiliation network to reflect on professional and political logics behind actions from the financial reform expert groups.

FRACTAL DISTINCTIONS

We follow Abbott's (2001) suggestion that fractal distinctions provide a useful tool for the analysis of disagreements. Abbott's starting point is that self-similarity in social systems is an important phenomenon and provides insight into how knowledge is transferred across groups and generations. Self-similarity provides a key means for the replication of identities and cultures, and is fundamental within social networks and communities (Padgett 2012). For fractal distinctions the basic concept is that, like geometric fractals, the distinctions replicate themselves in successive iterations, and that distinctions are important to identify synchronically and diachronically. The form of analysis has been applied to the study of conflicts among professional groups, including Abbott's (2001) study of sociology, Tarrow's (2008) investigation into political science, and Shwed and Bearman's (2010) work on scientific consensus formation. We apply it here to financial reform expert groups because many similar elements are present, including professionals 'straddling the fence' in their need to demonstrate professional autonomy while also serving a particular client base and principal (Larson 1977: 196). In short, fractal distinctions provide a useful way to study differentiation and conflicts among professional groups and to locate not only the sources of why distinctions are asserted, but also why they return.

To illustrate the concept of fractal distinctions we draw directly from Abbott's (2001) example of methodological factions in sociology. The argument is that if you have a group of sociologists in a room and ask them about method, they will quickly break down into quantitative and qualitative scholars. Ask again within these two groups and the respondents will most likely divide further, with some more quantitatively inclined asserting the need for greater quantitative depth (as with those focusing on regression analysis), and others stressing how quantitative methods must be supplemented with qualitative methods to provide greater context to explain behaviour (as with those using clustering methods). Take this division one step further and the same distinction between quantitative and qualitative methods will re-emerge, with the groups dividing themselves even further. One could make the same groups split into fractals by asking questions about 'history vs culture' or 'economy vs society' or 'economics vs politics'.

Fractal distinctions differ from traditional differentiation over issues, where there is increasingly specificity, because they revert to conflict between two ideas. The distinctions have to be supported by effort and resources among those who seek to maintain the importance of making a new iteration, or one of the distinctions may be rendered 'sterile', with a possibility of being 'remapped' later when the missing component is then viewed as essential (Abbott 2001: 22–3). Fractal distinctions are synchronic in shining a light on how groups differ from a distinction in a snapshot, as well as diachronically in that an idea linked to original distinctions will encounter greater abstraction and slippage, as well as rediscovery from the need for clarification about what exactly the distinction should mean (Abbott 2001: 10, 27). The long history of 'bringing something back in' is based on the reappearance of such fractal distinctions (most recently, Schmidt [2009]). Such debates rely on correcting an overemphasis on one element by reintroducing the other distinction.

We can easily identify a range of fractal distinctions linked to financial systems. During the last century, debates over how to regulate and structure the financial system have split over public/private, national/international and segmented/universal (Verdier 2003). These distinctions replicate themselves in debates over financial reform in the United States and in Europe during the twentieth century through periods of regulation, deregulation and reregulation. While distinctions such as segmentation/universal are adequate, we suggest that the fractal distinction most prominent during the recent crisis and evident in the reports of financial reform expert groups is behaviour/structure. We derive this distinction from the character of the debates on financial regulation in general and a close study of the recommendations. Behaviour and structure are replicated over time in financial reform debates, and through our inductive reasoning from assessments of the reports, the behaviour vs structure distinction is the key axis of difference. We find that the behaviour/structure fractal distinctions are evident at the different levels of the financial reform agenda. For example, a focus on banks as a unit ultimately covers recommendations targeting both behaviour (capital requirements, bonus structures) and structure (too big to fail, utility vs investment banking).

This kind of distinction can also be inherent in how different groups view conflicts in financial reform. For example, Simone Polillo's (2013) work on 'conservatives vs wildcats' conflicts highlights how conservatives rely on exclusionary tactics and politics that put forward notions of behavioural standards for 'sound finance', while wildcats seek to expand credit access through structural changes to the financial system that are inclusionary and introduce new financial institutions and practices. In Daniel Mügge's (2010) study of European financial market integration, there is a similar, if implicit, distinction, with securities firms seeking structural reforms to broaden their access to European markets, while also supporting the erection of high levels of entry to new firms, based on behavioural attributes.

The expert groups we study in this contribution differ strongly in whether the main object of regulation should be the behaviour of financial institutions or the structure of the financial system. The reports all provide a logic for financial reform that divides over behaviour or structure and then replicates the distinction to discuss different aspects of regulation that should be considered. Figure 1 outlines the basic distinctions. Those who follow one distinction persistently demonstrate extreme characteristics (*structure>structure>structure*, for example), which we comment on below. Our analysis shows that the extreme positions are uncommon and that most reports provide a mix of behaviour and structure thinking for reasons strongly associated with maintaining professional reputation.

Those working in expert groups have a clear incentive to make sure they are not dismissed as extremists, while also addressing the intended policy audience

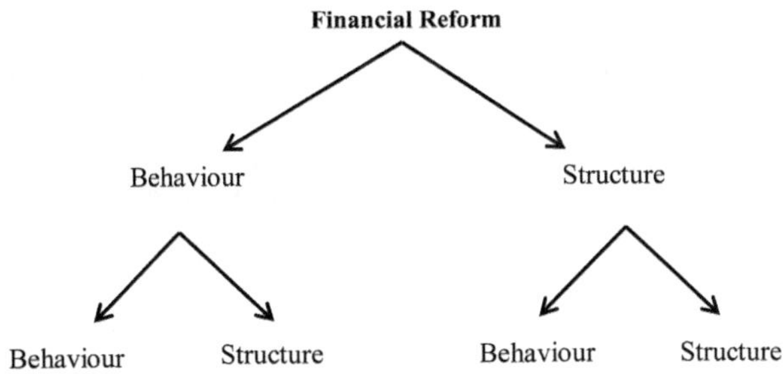

Figure 1 Fractal distinctions on financial reform

with a clear position. The professionals involved have an incentive to retain credibility among their peers in the transnational policy community, and ensure that they have both future work and esteem; they must also differentiate themselves from other groups in their policy proposals. We find, however, that this incentive to differentiate ultimately leads to a great deal of convergence on the issues considered relevant for reform. We return to the issue of professional logics after detailing how the behaviour/structure fractal distinction plays out from 11 financial reform expert group reports.

FRACTAL DISTINCTIONS IN FINANCIAL REFORM EXPERT GROUPS

For the purposes of our analysis, we identified 11 reports from 2008–2009. The reasoning behind this selection is twofold. First, we deliberately limited the time range to the initial crisis period: this helps us identify both the broad debates that were understood to be relevant for the crisis as it developed, but also the types of groups which were either mandated or self-selected to provide analysis and recommendations. We find that reports published from 2010 are, with few exceptions, much more likely to be contributing to 'agreed debates' than introducing new ideas. Second, we selected the specific 11 on the basis of financial media coverage (all were the subject of debate in *The Economist* and the major financial press), frequency of reference in interviews with the transnational policy community, and a final case integrity evaluation with selected policy officials.

We looked in detail at the following: intergovernmental reports by the Financial Stability Forum (FSF 2008), the International Monetary Fund (IMF 2009) and the United Nations (UN) Commission of Experts on Reforms of the International Monetary and Financial Systems (United Nations 2009); reports commissioned by the European Commission and national governments, specifically those of the De Larosière report of the High Level Group on Financial Supervision in the European Union (EU) (2009), the Financial Services Authority's Turner Review (FSA 2009) and the US Treasury (2009); reports by research organizations and policy clubs, namely the Geneva Report (Brunnermeier *et al.* 2009), the report of the Group of Thirty (G30 2009) and the Warwick Commission on International Financial Reform (2009); and reports produced by the private sector, the Institute of International Finance (IIF 2008) and the Counterparty Risk Management Policy Group (CRMPG 2009). Of those reports, all but the IMF, US Treasury and Turner Review documents have identifiable authors or working group members.

All of the reports reviewed offer a mix of analysis and recommendations that cover elements pertaining to both behaviour and structure. The degree of emphasis, detail of analysis and provision of concrete reform proposals vary a great deal. Among the intergovernmental efforts, for example, the FSF report (2008) places much emphasis on questions of improving the accuracy of valuation, and addresses issues of prudential oversight of behaviour-level activity. It does not neglect the global institutional framework, but the recommendations there are more about enabling existing arrangements to work well rather than reforming them. By contrast, the IMF report (2009) is strong on detail in relation to systemic questions, including early warning systems, surveillance, cross-border activities and co-ordination of macroprudential regulation. More wide-ranging still is the report of the UN Commission (UN 2009) which addresses controversial instruments and the size of financial institutions, while also suggesting new international organizations for global financial governance. This report also stands out for its analysis of global development questions associated with the crisis, including in relation to tax.

More detail can be found in the reports commissioned at the European and national levels. The De Larosière report (2009) offers a comprehensive and concrete reform agenda on questions of microprudential regulation, valuation, risk management, products and instruments; its main focus, however, is to rationalize European-level regulatory and supervisory arrangements, enabling a framework that can match the realities of cross-border financial institutions and activities. The report is much quieter on big structure questions, though it does refer to perennial 'European' concerns about hedge funds and tax havens. The report, expressly commissioned, has a clear mandate to produce recommendations that can be implementable, which further enhances the behaviour angle. The US Treasury report (2009) emphasizes the same set of issues, but also proves innovative, with proposals on consolidating regulatory and supervisory arrangements and on the resolution of large institutions. Its foray into structure issues lends support to macroprudential thinking (though with little detail) and shows concern for shadow banking and the effects on the real economy. The Turner Review (FSA 2009) too provides detailed technical recommendations on the behaviour questions, but also places considerable emphasis on macroprudential regulation and shadow banking, discusses the separation of banking into utility and investment components and addresses home–host regulation.

Research organizations and policy clubs go further in their structure-focused recommendations. The Geneva report (Brunnermeier *et al.* 2009) is full of technical detail on several behaviour-specific issues, but concentrates especially on segmentation, macroprudential regulation and different ways to think through products and instruments. The G30 report (2009) places similar emphasis on the last two questions and moves further on reforming the global financial governance framework, including through the separation of utility and investment banking. The Warwick Commission report (2009) focuses almost exclusively on structure issues, especially segmentation, macroprudential regulation and home–host country regulation.

Finally, the reports by the two private sector groups are both quite narrow in their focus on behaviour, but while the IIF (2008) provides recommendations related to better using existing financial regulation, the CRMPG (2008) is comprehensive on technical detail for deeper reform, especially with respect to risk management and the treatment of specific products and instruments.

The reports were coded to reveal emphasis on behaviour and structure in the financial reform proposals outlined in executive summaries and the full report texts. We surveyed the recommendations and scored them for emphasis on behaviour and structure according to the presence of particular categories. We also noted where recommendations on a particular issue were judged to be more radical in departing from the status quo. For 'behaviour', we reviewed recommendations for content on: incentives/compensation; risk management; valuation; and microprudential capital requirements. For 'structure', we examined recommendations for content on: utility vs investment banking; segmentation; macroprudential regulation; home–host regulation; shadow banking; tax havens; and a broader macroeconomic viewpoint. Additionally, we found recommendations relating to: resolution; products and instruments; and global regulatory arrangements and surveillance, which are not clearly about behaviour or structure and represent a mix of regulatory emphases. We coded them in a middle category, as can be seen in Table 1, which summarizes our reading of the reports' recommendations according to a behaviour/structure focus.

From a close reading, it is possible to ascertain the logic placed in each report to make each contribution to the debate distinctive. Those in the transnational policy community engaged in financial reform expert groups did not develop their reports in isolation. While there are clear questions of visibility, timing and authority in who were leaders among the groups, ideas were being developed and discussed both within and across groups. Within these networks, the extent of product differentiation was an important question asked by interlocutors in transnational and national policy communities during feedback and evidence sessions.[4]

We present the fractal distinctions in Figure 2, which distinguishes the reports in terms of behaviour and structure thinking on financial reform. The diagram flows over time, following the logic developed in the reports. Our coding and placement of the reports into the fractal distinctions follow the debates during 2008–2009, with the early reports represented at the top of the fractal and the later reports assessed in the distinctions below. The top half of the figure depicts reports that emerged in 2008 and early 2009, while the bottom half shows those that emerged in the second iteration of reports later

Table 1 Differentiating financial reform expert group policy recommendations

	Incentives/ compensation	*Risk management*	*Valuation*	*Microprudential capital requirements*	*Resolution*	*Products and instruments*	*Global regulatory arrangements/*	*Surveillance*	*Utility vs investment banking*	*Segmentation*	*Macroprudential regulation*	*Home–host regulation*	*Shadow banking*	*Tax havens*	*Macro context*
	Behaviour				*Behaviour/structure*					*Structure*					
FSF			X	X	X		X								
IMF					X*		X*				X				X
UN		X				X*	X*			X				X	X*
De Larosière	X	X	X	X	X	X	X*				X		X	X	
Turner	X	X	X	X	X	X			X		X*	X*	X*	X	
US Treasury	X	X	X	X	X	X	X				X		X		X
Geneva	X		X	X		X*				X*	X*	X			
G30		X	X	X	X	X*	X*		X*		X*		X		
Warwick					X*	X				X*	X	X*			X*
IIF	X	X	X												
CRMPG		X*	X			X*									

Note: X denotes coverage of the issue; X* denotes greater emphasis and a comprehensive reform proposal.

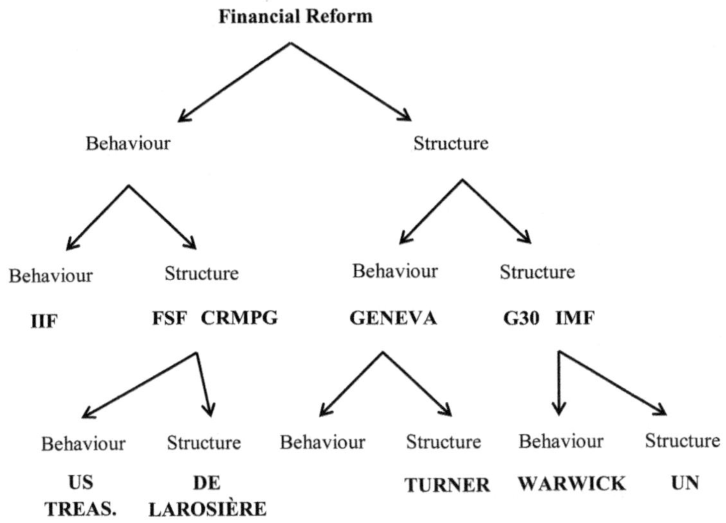

Figure 2 Fractal distinctions in financial reform expert groups

in 2009. As participant observers in these debates, we found that the flow of knowledge about what could be legitimately included in financial regulation came from previous reports, ongoing debates and the professional interactions of expert group participants. Over time this reaffirmed the distinctions identified and then, in the second iteration, led to further cleavages in stress over what was important to reform, as well as what reform ideas were marketable. The reports have been coded to show how the fractals are replicated over time, and we have matched the most similar reports over time, stressing how they break in their emphasis on behaviour or structure. Given that this is a reasonably close-knit professional community of financial reform experts, debates and reports in earlier rounds do inform debates and reports in subsequent rounds. While it is tempting to view the collapse of Lehman Brothers and other spectacular events during the crisis as having led to radical changes in thinking (*cf.* Moschella and Tsingou 2013), following the reasoning in the reports and associated debates shows how thinking about financial reform stayed within the behaviour/structure distinctions.

As with the fractal distinctions previously discussed, the behaviour/structure distinction is repeated in the development of the reports, with some distinctions becoming 'sterile' for the time being. From Figure 2 it is clear that the reports vary widely in their emphasis but still replicate the distinction. The IIF provides an extreme example where the object of regulation and the recommendations follow behaviour thinking only, with their emphasis on incentives and compensation, risk management and valuation of banks. This emphasis on behaviour is not replicated in the last round of reports. At the other extreme, the UN report provides structure-level thinking all the way down, including 'blue sky' thinking about the structure of the financial system with vague detail on policy implementation.

The national and regional commissioned reports provide the most complex formulations. The US Treasury report (*behaviour>structure>behaviour*) covers a broad range of issues, including questions of architecture and infrastructure, but its initial and ultimate focus is on detailed recommendations for altering behaviour. The Turner Review is the most elaborate on the structure side (*structure>behaviour>structure*), moving from a discussion about the role of the financial sector in society, to questions that should be addressed by technical recommendations, to broader issues such as macroprudential regulation, and separating banking into utility and investment components. The De Larosière report starts with a more explicit set of recommendations on behaviour but expands on structural elements (*behaviour>structure>structure*) as they relate to the rationalization of European-wide and cross-country financial activities.

It is noteworthy that there is a great deal of difference among the reports, while advocates for significant change on issues such as shadow banking, tax havens and home–host regulation are in the minority. We suggest that the reason is that the distinctions made reflect the interests of the transnational policy community engaged in the work, as well as the institutions supporting them. We turn first to the professional context in which work on financial reform expert groups was conducted.

PROFESSIONAL LOGICS IN FINANCIAL REFORM EXPERT GROUPS

Work on the financial reform expert groups was conducted by professionals with experience in the international public and private sectors and who specialize in financial regulation and governance.[5] Those chairing the groups were well-known names in the transnational policy community on financial governance, as can be seen in Table 2.

Those named chaired the expert groups, and staffing followed similar lines. It is important to note that the life of the financial reform expert group and the careers of those involved have different horizons. The crisis event generated the demand for the expert groups from various authorities, and those selected to chair the groups were drawn from established leaders in the area of financial governance, as well as those with policy ideas clearly worked out prior to the 2007 crisis (Persaud 2000). Given that the transnational policy community is close-knit, one could expect different forms of blocking and brokering behaviour, as is common in all social networks. Professionals are often interested in maintaining their established position by blocking access to certain tasks through 'jurisdictional' battles to ensure that other professions and professionals are not permitted to work on the problem at hand (Abbott 1988). Brokers, on the other hand, have an interest in spreading their ideas and knowledge between non-connected actors and will seek to carve out their own professional space to

Table 2 Chairs of financial reform expert groups

Commission	*Chair*
CRMPG	Corrigan
De Larosière	De Larosière
Geneva	NA
Group of Thirty	Volcker
FSA	Turner
FSF	Draghi
IIF	Waugh (co-chair)
IIF	Maas (co-chair)
IMF	NA
UN	Stiglitz
US Treasury	Geithner
Warwick	Persaud

ensure their place in the network or, in our case, the transnational policy community (*cf.* Goddard 2009). These dynamics also map onto different career styles, such as technocrats and brokers (Seabrooke 2011), and provide a source of professional competition within the community. The use of professional knowledge in financial reform expert groups also follows these dynamics, with the fractal distinctions discussed above being maintained because they demarcate the boundaries of the relevant policy audience (though not necessary politicians or publics).

To assess how professionals who are working group members are linked to different financial reform expert groups, we present a simple affiliation network in Figure 3. The diagram locates the authors (grey circles) and their relationship with the reports in this study for which the working teams are named (white squares for those reports favouring behaviour and black squares for those reports favouring structure). The point of the affiliation network is to see how working group members and authors are related to one another through common participation in reports (Field *et al.* 2006). While we acknowledge arguments about the homogeneity of thinking among the transnational policy community, this allows us to detect when the same authors are involved in very different reform suggestions.

As can be seen from Figure 3, there are four common working group members in the G30 and IIF reports. If one returns to the relevant sections of Table 1 and Figure 2, it is clear that the policy recommendations from these two reports differ strongly. As will be elaborated upon in the following section, there are very distinct settings in which the transnational policy community operates, and where expectations and audiences differ accordingly. The dynamics present in affiliation networks are, of course, not only present in financial governance. As Woody Powell and his collaborators have identified in their study of interorganizational collaboration in the life sciences:

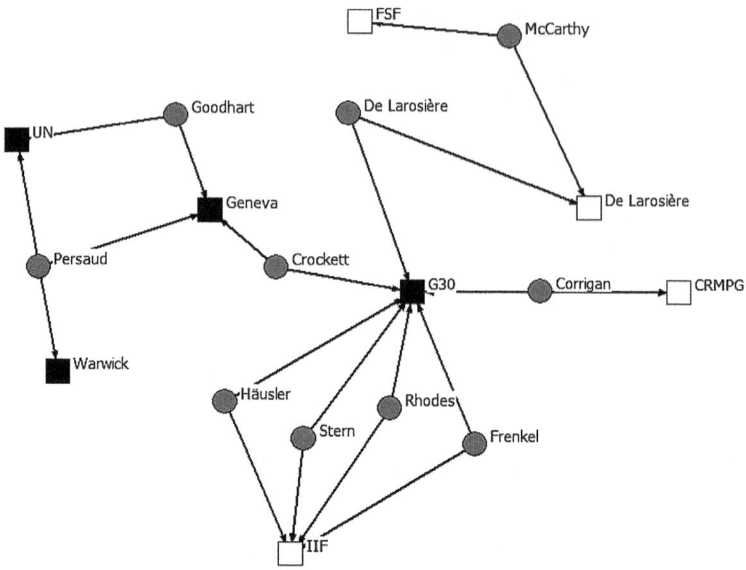

Figure 3 Affiliation network of financial reform expert group members

> The pattern of cross-cutting collaborations often results in a partner on one project being a rival on another. The frequent rewiring of attachments means that participants have to learn how to exit from relationships gracefully so as not to damage future prospects for affiliation. In a system where external sources of knowledge and resources are widely differentiated, a preference for diversity and affiliation with multiconnected partners has mobilizing consequences.
>
> (Powell *et al.* 2005: 1187)

The same logic applies to professionals and their use of professional knowledge in financial reform expert groups. Given the incentives for maintaining a positive relationship with the transnational policy community, membership of the community supports the replication of fractal distinctions such as behaviour and structure because affirming the importance of existing distinctions permits room for differentiation to constituencies while also maintaining a position among peers that does not impinge on future work. It is no surprise then that those identified as radicals in the transnational policy community seek to augment their position by allying themselves with professionals from different professional ecologies (Seabrooke and Tsingou 2009). For example, Andrew Haldane, the executive director for financial stability at the Bank of England, has found credibility and prestige for his ideas about financial systems as fragile ecosystems from his engagement with epidemiology, biology and engineering, including co-authoring an article in *Nature* with a zoologist (Haldane and May 2011). Such positions would be identified as radical in the framework depicted above in Figure 2 and not included in reports that seek to address a policy audience in the short term; the professional strategy on thinking about financial systems as ecosystems may reflect a long-term goal to shape policy thinking.[6]

Looking specifically at the authors of the reports in our study, we also find that Avinash Persaud's position in the network in Figure 3 is of particular interest for his brokering between the Geneva, UN, and Warwick reports. Persaud's brokerage role could be understood as making him an 'issue entrepreneur' seeking to propagate a particular set of ideas and values (Carpenter 2011), such as 'home–host regulation' in the Geneva and Warwick reports, and 'segmentation' in all three reports, as can be seen in Table 1. This entrepreneurial action includes some 'epistemic arbitrage' in moving between different professional groups to affirm what knowledge is appropriate in reform discussions (Seabrooke 2014). Persaud's brokerage role can be distinguished from the technocrats linking the G30 and IIF reports, whose work focused on different aspects of financial reform, depending on the setting and audience. In contrast to 'issue entrepreneurs', these individuals can be characterized as 'issue professionals' in being concerned with esteem and prestige among peers in the professional community rather than advocacy of certain positions.

DISTINCTIONS AND AFFILIATIONS IN FINANCIAL REFORM EXPERT GROUPS

We noted above that the IIF (2008) and G30 (2009) reports focused, respectively, exclusively on behaviour and on structure, the latter endorsing macroprudential regulation and discussing the separation of utility and investment banking. We can also note that from Figure 2 the extreme position on the left (all behaviour) disappears over time and that the left and right (all structure) of the diagram reflect different authority relations. On the left side of the diagram is the IIF, an international lobby group seeking to contain regulatory costs for its members, the banks. On the right hand side is a mix of groups. The G30 produced a financial grandee report which showed reform ambition and tested the waters for the ideas of key brokers such as Paul Volcker. The IMF staff (2009) produced a report with no names attached, no executive board authority, and with the knowledge that concrete recommendations that isolated some of its members would cause trouble (Seabrooke 2012). As such the IMF report was a demonstration of technocratic expertise, and perhaps bureaucratic autonomy, with no political teeth. The report most focused on structure by the UN group (2009) covered the widest range of macro areas and was reformist without being especially concrete. The two extreme positions reflect, first, unaccountability of the IIF to a constituency beyond its members. On the other side, they show IMF and UN accountability in providing seemingly equal treatment to all of their members and the relative freedom of self-appointed groups to decide upon their audience.

The relationship between distinctions in financial reform expert groups and the authority behind the groups tells us something about the use of professional knowledge and the character of the transnational policy community. First, it is clear that there is no ownership of ideas on financial reform, as authors and working group members move between different reports. Understanding their actions as technocrats and brokers makes more sense, given that they seek to secure their professional position in the community while also customizing the presentation of reform proposals for defined audiences. Indeed, we suggest that the key differences in financial reform expert groups can be explained by the authority behind the commissioning and the extent to which there is a defined audience for the project.

Table 3 locates the financial reform expert groups under study by how they came into existence and their audience. The Warwick Commission report (2009) was self-funded and used its independence to make its mark in contributing a political economy approach to financial reform debates. As can be seen in Table 1, the report strongly pushed the idea of home versus host country regulation, a proposal for the reform of the international financial architecture adopted by the also self-appointed Geneva report (Brunnermeier *et al.* 2009) in a milder form (recall that Persaud served on both expert groups). Professional knowledge in this environment seeks to differentiate ideas and reform proposals compared to groups that have been especially commissioned for a purpose by a political authority, or those that have a clear mandate to provide an international public good with the backing of states (or private banks, as is the case with IIF). We find that the categorizations in Table 3 help us to explain the silences in the financial reform debate, such as the lack of engagement with issues like tax havens and shadow banking. There are, perhaps, good reasons why tax havens were commonly left out of the reports, given that addressing them required political clout rather than professional innovation, while the initial post-crisis discussions on macroprudential regulation provided a significant intellectual challenge.

Among the expert groups with a defined audience, we can also see that the ones with a national/regional origin and perspective are the least extreme and most complex. As Figure 2 shows, the report by the US Treasury (2009), the Turner Review (FSA 2009) and the De Larosière exercise (2009) cover a range of issues across behaviour and structure. This is indicative of a concern for plausible implementation. The De Larosière report was a concrete reform

Table 3 Authorities and audiences

	Defined audience	*Non-defined audience*
Mandate	FSF, US Treasury, Turner, IIF	IMF
Commission	De Larosière	UN
Self-appointment	CRMPG	Geneva, G30, Warwick

plan that could be at least partially adopted during the 'hot' period without stumbling into delays over policy applicability. However, although there are some national and regional elements in the three reports, they are not linked to national interests but, rather, national and regional considerations of effectiveness (the regulatory authority has to match the geographical market). The reports are still part of a field, and some individual recommendations closely resemble each other.

Given the mix of professional competition to create distinct ideas within the transnational policy community, the need to respond to particular constituencies (Tsingou 2013), and the absence of consensus on issues such as what macroprudential regulation should look like, the lack of radical reform on the big structure questions in global financial governance can be explained. This could be expected, in particular, from reports where the scope of recommendations and the broadness of the audience require decisive action to be taken by a central authority that is unable to foster agreement among all constituents. Such dynamics can be seen with the De Larosière report (2009), where European members of the transnational policy community suggested that it provided a big step forward for the European project.[7] But while praising the report's linkages from micro to macro, it was also acknowledged that it amounted to connecting the national to the European level, with less attention to global systemic questions.[8] On this issue of structure-level reform, the EU would require a common voice in global financial governance, which has not yet happened (Mügge 2011).

CONCLUSION

We suggest that fractal distinctions are a useful way to analyse conflicts in professional groups, in our case those working with financial reform expert groups in 2008–2009. Our findings detail how the reports produced during this period differ in their combination of addressing the object of regulation, the behaviour or the structure, and how sequences of behaviour and structure thinking can be seen in the detailed report recommendations. We suggest the distinctions made among the reports are political in that they reflect different constituencies, mandates and audiences. A simple analysis of the affiliation network associated with expert groups where the authors are clearly named shows how close-knit this transnational policy community is and, importantly, how affiliations are not directly tied to the fractal distinctions. One can work on an expert group report that reflects behaviour thinking, as well as on one that is dominated by thinking about the structure. One can also act as a broker and engage in 'epistemic arbitrage' to exploit structural holes between disconnected professionals in financial reform expert groups and have influence in different organizational contexts (Seabrooke 2014). As we have seen above, there are numerous incentives for members of the transnational policy community to protect their access to ongoing professional work while also seeking to distinguish themselves, and their reports, to influence the debate within this community.

We argue that comparing fractal distinctions in the reports with the affiliation network highlights how the report recommendations are not the properties of individuals working in the expert groups. Rather, the proposed policy reform ideas are linked to those commissioning the work and the constituencies the relevant groups should target. This is to be expected in 'hot' periods of knowledge production, where there is a policy audience, politicians and publics waiting to hear how their concerns are being addressed. This behaviour conflicts with the club-like transnational policy community on financial governance, including professional jurisdictional behaviour that would prefer technical solutions to problems in financial systems to be addressed during 'cold' periods of knowledge production (Callon 1998). It also moves away from expectations that national and regional interests and specificities would drive the reform agenda.

Finally, we have pointed to how thinking about fractal distinctions provides a tool for investigating professional conflicts and distinguishing differences and trends in debates. We have placed emphasis on what the distinctions tell us in terms of incentives for professionals to stay within their transnational policy community. As a tool, fractal distinctions are also useful in highlighting silent issues, such as the lack of engagement with shadow banking in the studied reports. While dismissing false dichotomies has become the bread and butter for academics and policy-makers alike, investigating how distinctions are repeatedly invoked provides a window into seeing how systems of professional knowledge and interaction are maintained.

Biographical note: Leonard Seabrooke is professor of international political economy and economy sociology at the Copenhagen Business School. Eleni Tsingou is assistant professor of international political economy at the Copenhagen Business School.

ACKNOWLEDGEMENTS

This research was funded by the 'Professions in International Political Economies' project from the European Research Council (#263741-PIPES). We thank Andrew Baker, Shogo Suzuki and participants to the 'EU in Global Financial Governance' workshop for their valuable feedback.

NOTES

1 Authors' interview, Confederation of British Industry (June 2009).

2 Author interviews, G30 report working group participant (February 2010) and Bank of England (October 2009).
3 Leonard Seabrooke directed the Warwick Commission and Eleni Tsingou was a Commissioner. We recognize that this report does not carry the same weight as reports commissioned or sanctioned by formal organizations. We include it not only for the insights into the professional dynamics of expert group writing, but also because of coverage in the financial press, including an article directly comparing it to the Bank of England's position and a report on key ideas for systemic reform in *The Economist* (2009, 2010).
4 Authors' participant observation. The Warwick Commission met three times prior to writing the report (January, March and June 2009). Additionally, the authors organized evidence sessions with public officials and practitioners in London (May–June 2009).
5 The Warwick Commission differed as it was half composed of political scientists, including prominent academics in the study of finance in the international political economy, such as Mark Blyth and Eric Helleiner.
6 Author interviews, US White House economic advisor (February 2009) and Bank of England (May 2009).
7 Author interview, Oesterreichische Nationalbank (May 2009).
8 Author interview, De Larosière report group member (May 2009).

REFERENCES

Abbott, A. (1988) *The System of Professions*, Chicago, IL: University of Chicago Press.
Abbott, A. (2001) *Chaos of Disciplines*, Chicago, IL: University of Chicago Press.
Baker, A. (2013) 'The new political economy of the macroprudential ideational shift', *New Political Economy* 18(1): 112–39.
Brunnermeier, M. *et al.* (2009) 'The fundamental principles of financial regulation', *Geneva Reports on the World Economy* 11, Geneva: International Center for Monetary and Banking Studies.
Callon, M. (1998) 'An essay on framing and overflowing: economic externalities revisited by Sociology', in M. Callon (ed.), *The Laws of the Market*, Oxford: Blackwell, pp. 244–69.
Carpenter, R.C. (2011) 'Vetting the advocacy agenda: networks, centrality and the paradox of weapons norms', *International Organization* 65(1): 69–102.
Counterparty Risk Management Policy Group (2008) *Containing Systemic Risk: The Road to Reform. The Report of the CRMPG III*, 6 August, available at http://cdm16064.contentdm.oclc.org/cdm/ref/collection/p266901coll4/id/2422 (accessed February 2014).
De Larosière Group (2009) *Report of the High Level Group on Financial Supervision in the EU*, Brussels.
The Economist (2009) Systems failure', 26 November.
The Economist (2010) 'Special report on financial risk', 11 February.
Field, S., Frank, K.A., Schiller, K., Riegle-Crumb, C. and Muller, C. (2006) 'Identifying positions from affiliation networks: preserving the duality of people and events', *Social Networks* 28(2): 97–123.
Financial Services Authority (2009) *The Turner Review*, London: FSA.
Financial Stability Forum (2008) *Report on Enhancing Market and Institutional Resilience*, Basel: FSF.
Goddard, S. (2009) 'Brokering change: networks and entrepreneurs in international politics', *International Theory* 1(2): 249–81.
Group of Thirty (2009) *Financial Reform: A Framework for Financial Stability*, Washington, DC: G30.

Haldane, A.G. and May, R.M. (2011) 'System risk in banking ecosystems', *Nature* 469: 351–5.

Helleiner, E., Pagliari, S. and Zimmermann, H. (eds) (2009) *Global Finance in Crisis*, London: Routledge.

Institute of International Finance (2008) *Final Report of the IIF Committee on Market Best Practices: Principles of Conduct and Best Practice Recommendations*, Washington, DC: IIF.

International Monetary Fund (2009) *Initial Lessons of the Crisis for the Global Architecture and the IMF*, Washington, DC: IMF.

Larson, M.S. (1977) *The Rise of Professionalism*, Berkeley, CA: University of California Press.

Moschella, M. and Tsingou, E. (2013) (eds) *Great Expectations, Slow Transformations*, Colchester: ECPR Press.

Mügge, D. (2010) *Widen the Market, Narrow the Competition*, Colchester: ECPR Press.

Mügge, D. (2011) 'The European presence in global financial governance: a principal–agent perspective', *Journal of European Public Policy* 18(3): 383–402.

Padgett, J.F. (2012) 'From chemical to social networks', in J.F. Padgett and W.W. Powell (eds), *The Emergence of Organizations and Markets*, Princeton, NJ: Princeton University Press, pp. 92–114.

Persaud, A. (2000) 'Sending the herd off the cliff edge: the disturbing interaction between herding and market-sensitive risk management practices', *Journal of Risk Finance* 2(1): 59–65.

Polillo, S. (2013) *Conservatives vs Wildcats*, Palo Alto, CA: Stanford University Press.

Powell, W.W., White, D.R., Koput, K.W. and Smith, J.O. (2005) 'Network dynamics and field evolution: the growth of interorganizational collaboration in the Life Sciences', *American Journal of Sociology* 110(4): 1132–205.

Quaglia, L. (2014) 'The sources of European Union influence in international financial regulatory fora', *Journal of European Public Policy*.

Seabrooke, L. (2011) 'Economists and diplomacy: professions and the practice of economic policy', *International Journal* LXVI(Summer): 629–42.

Seabrooke, L. (2012) 'Pragmatic numbers: the IMF, financial reform, and policy learning in least likely environments', *Journal of International Relations and Development* 15(4): 486–505.

Seabrooke, L. (2014) 'Epistemic arbitrage: transnational professional knowledge in action', *Journal of Professions and Organizations* 1(1), doi: 10.1093/jpo/jot005.

Seabrooke, L. and Tsingou, E. (2009) 'Revolving doors and linked ecologies in the world economy: policy locations and the practice of international financial reform', *Working Paper 260*. Coventry: CSGR.

Schmidt, V.A. (2009) 'Putting the political back into political economy by bringing the state back in yet again', *World Politics* 61(3): 516–46.

Shwed, U. and Bearman, P.S. (2010) 'The temporal structure of scientific consensus formation', *American Sociological Review* 75(6): 817–40.

Tarrow, S. (2008) 'Polarization and convergence in academic controversies', *Theory and Society* 37(6): 513–36.

Tsingou, E. (2013) 'Transnational veto players and the practice of financial reform', *British Journal of Politics and International Relations*, doi: 10.1111/1467-856X.12031.

United Nations (2009) *UN Commission of Experts on Reforms of the International Monetary and Financial Systems, Recommendations*, New York: United Nations.

US Treasury (2009) *Financial Regulatory Reform – A New Foundation: Rebuilding Financial Supervision and Regulation*, Washington, DC: US Treasury.

Verdier, D. (2003) *Moving Money*, Cambridge: Cambridge University Press.

Warwick Commission on International Financial Reform (2009) *In Praise of Unlevel Playing Fields*, Coventry: University of Warwick.

Experimentalism in European Union and global financial governance: interactions, contrasts, and implications

Malcolm Campbell-Verduyn and Tony Porter

ABSTRACT Evidence of substantial experimental governance has been found in a variety of areas of European Union (EU) governance. However the relationship between experimentalism in the EU and global governance remains unclear. Is experimentalist governance an advantage or a disadvantage for the EU in its interactions with global regulatory arrangements? This contribution examines the experimentalist character of EU financial governance and its interactions with the International Monetary Fund, the Basel Committee on Banking Supervision and the International Financial Reporting Standards governance institutions. Our analysis suggests that experimentalism provides advantages for the EU in areas of global governance that are themselves experimentalist. This argument challenges more conventional approaches that view bureaucratically centralized power as always necessary for the successful promotion of interests and attainment of influence at the global level. Since some governance problems require detailed harmonized rule implementation at single points in time, we also find that experimentalist variation occurs temporally as well as across locations or jurisdictions.

Experimentalist governance (EG), as identified by Charles Sabel and Jonathan Zeitlin, involves the setting of general revisable framework goals, the encouragement of multiple types of rule-making to achieve those goals, measures to gauge their achievement, a rigorous process of reporting and peer evaluation to determine what works best, as well as mechanisms for revising the goals, measures and rules. Evidence of substantial experimentalism has been found in a variety of areas of European Union (EU) governance (Sabel and Zeitlin 2010b) and in some global settings (De Búrca *et al.* 2013; Nance and Cottrell 2013). However, the relationship between experimentalism in the EU and in global governance remains unclear.

There are good reasons to expect that the objectives of the EU will be harmed in its global interactions by the adoption of EG in internal policy processes. Interactions at the global level have traditionally been seen to involve power politics among centralized states competing in an anarchic setting characterized by relatively ineffective formal international organizations and laws. This traditional type of world politics is likely to be inhospitable to experimentalism. Not only does experimentalism require more flexible integration than this type of world politics provides, but traditional theories have assumed that centralized unified states are the only form of organization that is likely to survive anarchic power politics. Therefore, we might expect the EU to be weakened in its global interactions by its own experimentalism.

Contrary to this view, we argue that experimentalism benefits the EU in its global interactions. This is especially because an increasing number of global settings have experimentalist elements, and the EU's own experimentalism provides benefits for interactions in such global settings. Yet EG is not a self-contained system that confronts or wholly replaces alternatives such as centralized governance or anarchy. Instead, the emergence of EG should be understood as part of a much larger epochal shift from more traditional to more reflexive modes of governance, which cuts across all levels of analysis from the most macro global levels to micro levels below the nation-state. Experimentalism within the EU positions it to take better advantage of these changes than would centralized non-experimentalist policies in the EU or elsewhere. This is both because the EU can respond to the changes that are simultaneously driving experimentalism in the EU and globally, and because experimentalist EU practices interact in compatible ways with experimentalist elements in global governance.

While we think the logic of our argument, as developed below, is compelling, in this contribution we are only able to offer suggestive empirical support rather than definitive proof. We explore three cases of EU engagement with global financial governance, with varying degrees of experimentalism present in three different global level institutions: the International Monetary Fund (IMF); the Basel Committee on Banking Supervision (BCBS); and the International Financial Reporting Standards (IFRS) governance institutions associated with the International Accounting Standards Board (IASB). The IMF is a more formal organization characterized by power politics, while the BCBS and IFRS governance bodies hold significant experimentalist elements. We find that the more traditional setting of the former is one in which the EU has experienced diminishing returns in contrast to the greater benefits the 28-member Union has enjoyed in the more experimentalist settings of the latter global venues. However, global financial governance involves a high degree of complexity, and drawing definitive conclusions with more cases goes beyond the scope of this study.

This contribution begins with a conceptual discussion of EG prior to analysing the EU and global financial governance. We examine the character of experimentalism at the EU level before turning to our three cases of EU engagement with the IMF, the BCBS, and the IFRS governance bodies. The contribution concludes with a discussion of the implications of these arguments for future EU policy choices and its prospects in global governance.

GLOBAL EXPERIMENTALIST GOVERNANCE

Sabel and Zeitlin (2008, 2010a, 2010b, 2011) have identified the defining characteristics of a mode of governance that has become important in the EU, which they have labelled experimentalist governance. One of their valuable contributions is to specify how the different components of EG work together to improve the flexibility, use of expertise and accountability of governance. Often such new and more complex forms of governance are seen as problematic, as they move away from traditional procedural or legal means of holding decision-makers and experts accountable. However, Sabel and Zeitlin contend that these three contemporary demands can be reconciled in mutually reinforcing ways as competing rules and systematic evaluation procedures force authorities to engage in debates that facilitate scrutiny by and engagement with stakeholders.

The value of Sabel and Zeitlin's model has been enhanced by pertinent case studies of EG in the EU and elsewhere, including in global governance. EG has been characterized as 'rule making in national and global fora . . . beyond the ken of the "command and control" relations characteristic of the modern state' (Sabel and Zeitlin 2008: 304). Multiple forms of global EG regimes have been elaborated (Börzel 2012; Nance and Cottrell 2013; Overdevest and Zeitlin 2012: 6; Sabel and Zeitlin 2010a), as have the origins, conditions, avenues and conceptual issues associated with the emergence of EG processes beyond the nation state (Overdevest and Zeitlin 2012: 6; Sabel and Zeitlin 2008: 280–92, 2011: 14–17). Furthermore, experimentalism's contributions to the generation and legitimization of public and private global regulatory regimes have been elaborated (Brassett *et al.* 2012; De Búrca *et al.* 2013).

Despite the valuable insights provided by this literature, the distinctive interactions between EG in jurisdictions such as the EU with global governance more generally have not been adequately conceptualized. EG often is implicitly or explicitly viewed as displacing or competing with more traditional modes of governance at either the global or the EU levels. The cases in the most comprehensive published analysis of EG, Sabel and Zeitlin (2010b), all concern comparisons and tensions between EG and traditional governance within the EU. Similarly, the framework in which De Búrca *et al.* (2013) specify features of EG that can be observed in a number of emerging global-level regimes implicitly situates global EG regimes within a larger set of more traditional global regimes. Comparable approaches are taken by Brassett *et al.* (2012) and Nance and Cottrell (2013) in their respective analyses of the emergence of experimentalist elements in private governance schemes and security arrangements at the global level. Overdevest and Zeitlin (2012) usefully illustrate how the EU has been able to draw on its own power to encourage the emergence of experimentalist features in the global forestry regime (see also Sabel and Zeitlin 2011). Yet, is it the power of the EU that allows it to promote experimentalism globally, or is it the EU's adoption of experimentalism that grants it power?

To fill these gaps in EG theorizing, we propose two interconnected revisions. A first is to treat EG as part of a wider reflexive trend that sociologists have identified at all levels of contemporary life. The concept of reflexivity has been insightfully developed in the work on 'reflexive modernization' (Beck *et al.* 1994). As Giddens (1990: 38) has put it, 'the reflexivity of modern social life consists in the fact that social practices are continually examined and reformed in the light of incoming information about those very practices, thus constitutively altering their character'. Such changes are occurring at all scales:

> On the global level, therefore, modernity has become experimental . . . The global experiment of modernity intersects with, and influences as it is influenced by, the penetration of modern institutions into the tissue of day-to-day life. Not just the local community, but intimate features of personal life and the self become intertwined with relations of indefinite time-space extension. (Beck *et al.* 1994: 59)

Many aspects of reflexivity are present in EG as well. These include complexity, interdependence, social acceleration, flexibility and intensified monitoring and revision of practices, all of which can be counter-posed to more fixed, centralized and formal traditional governance arrangements. These changes have been widely recognized in varying ways by scholars studying global governance (Porter 2014).

Such wider epochal increase in experimentalism is important, as it makes it more likely that the EU will encounter compatible changes occurring elsewhere, instead of confronting hostile or incompatible environments that will render its experimentalism a liability. At the same time, treating experimentalism as a series of elements that can be present in less coherent forms than many of the cases that the EG literature identifies means that experimentalism can often be present in global settings in which traditional power politics persists.

Our second conceptual revision of EG stems from the global governance literature. Experimentation is seen in EG scholarship as reliant on variation that occurs as framework goals are simultaneously implemented in different ways. However, at the global level uneven implementation will often be associated with collective action pathologies such as unlevel competitive playing fields, free riding or the type of cross-border contagion that can occur in finance and elsewhere when non-compliant actors threaten the stability of the system as a whole (Abbott and Snidal 2001). In such settings, we propose that the experimentalism may occur in a co-ordinated manner across time through the evaluation of a succession of harmonized implementation efforts, rather than by comparing simultaneous variation across implementation projects. Such *temporal* experimentation is consistent with the concept of learning in global governance, which has been distinguished from adaptation (Haas 1990; Haas and Haas 1995). Adaptation does not question underlying theories and values, as the emphasis is on means not ends, and new goals are added and dropped sequentially without integrating them conceptually into routines. In contrast, learning involves more profound questioning, reworking and integration into underlying beliefs.

How do the above conceptual revisions enable us to better understand the relationship between experimentalism in the EU and in global governance? We suggest that where elements of EG are present both globally as well as in the EU, the Union may derive benefits from closer interactions with these global institutions relative to other states or groupings of states that lack elements of experimentalism. The flexibility that experimentalism provides is likely to permit the EU to engage more thoroughly with the flexibility of EG in global settings. The role of experts associated with EG in the EU may facilitate the integration of policy ideas between the global and regional levels. Engagement and scrutiny from a range of stakeholders at the EU and global levels can also enhance the legitimacy and wider acceptance of policy outcomes generated through interactions between the EU and global mechanisms.

The EU should thus be better positioned to contribute to global rule-making in policy areas overseen by experimentalist global institutions. The EU should be better able to make use of whatever outputs the global rules produce more effectively than traditional centralized states or groupings of states. Moreover, the integration of global experiments into EU or national experiments should create leverage for the EU or experimentalist nation states, since the success of those global experiments will become relatively more reliant on those national or regional experiments for implementation (Newman and Bach 2014). Conversely, in more traditional settings characterized by the exercise of threats, coercion or bargaining, or more formal organizations and laws, the EU's experience with EG is likely to be less relevant.

EXPERIMENTALISM, THE EU AND GLOBAL FINANCIAL GOVERNANCE

In this section we begin with an overview of existing literature that considers the role of the EU in global financial governance. We then proceed to assess the experimentalist nature of EU and global financial governance institutions by the degree to which they display the capacity to reflexively alter rule formulation and implementation, consistent with the sociological literature, our temporal experimentalism and the initial criteria established by Sabel and Zeitlin (2008). Overall, we indicate how interactions with global level institutions exhibiting experimentalist elements provide advantages to the EU.

The existing literature

Literature on EU foreign policy is relatively small (Jørgensen 2009; Kissack 2010: 5) and scholarship on EU financial diplomacy is considerably thinner, though growing (Mügge forthcoming). Despite this scarcity, two contrasting approaches to analysing the roles of the EU in global financial governance can be identified.

A first approach emphasizes the alignment of member states preferences and centralized EU bargaining power. Overlapping member state interests are considered here as permitting negotiating capacity to be concentrated in either EU-level institutions or powerful member states in ways that provide 'European stakeholders . . . a good chance of figuring prominently on the global stage' (Mügge 2011: 384). Conversely, diverging member state preferences are viewed as leading to fragmented bargaining where 'no single party is empowered to negotiate' (*ibid.*: 390), and which in turn entails a 'limited reach and relevance' (*ibid.*: 391) for the EU in global fora. EU influence in global financial regulatory arrangements has similarly been attributed to its 'regulatory capacity' (Quaglia 2013) and 'cohesiveness' (Quaglia 2014). The EU here 'uploads' its rules to the global level when regional governance capabilities are strong, but is left to 'download' global rules when regional governance capacities remain weak. Although particular characteristics of global financial institutions, including their relative strengths and lengths of existence, also influence such 'uploading' or 'downloading' of governance elements to or from the global level, aligned state preferences and centralized bargaining power are considered to be the central determinants of the role of the EU in global financial governance. We can therefore think of this first approach as consistent with a non-experimentalist policy mode.

Meanwhile, an alternative approach considers the relevance of linkages between experimentalism in the EU and in global financial governance. Posner (n.d.) contends that global responses to the 2007–8 financial crisis involved clear shifts towards experimentalism. Elements of EG have included the reforms commonly agreed upon by 19 major nation states plus the EU at the Group of 20 (G20) whose decentralized domestic implementation involves deep mutual accountability through newly institutionalized informal mechanisms such as the Financial Stability Board's peer review and colleges of supervisors, rather than through formal bureaucratic organizations. Posner explores the degree to which experimentalism in global financial reforms has borrowed from EU experiences, finding weak links in the case of the Financial Stability Board's peer review process, but strong links in the case of colleges of supervisors.

Posner's contribution is valuable, as it begins to analyse the independent contribution that the character of global and EU institutions can make to the EU's role in global financial governance beyond the preferences, power and unity of member states. Yet Posner's analysis is of developments that are not systematically linked to variation in the character of global and EU financial governance institutions. The subsections that follow seek to provide this more systematic comparison.

Is the EU financial governance architecture experimentalist?

In this subsection we argue that, despite the centralization that has occurred since the most recent financial crisis began in 2007, EU financial governance retains significant elements of experimentalism. In contrast to the powerful nation states it interacts with in global settings, the EU's general structure remains one in which central EU institutions set frameworks and mechanisms for assessing the degree to which common goals are met, while implementation relies on relatively devolved mechanisms.

Experimentation in the EU financial governance architecture is particularly evident in the degree of institutional changes prior to and since the beginning of the financial crisis. The institutional evolution of the EU financial governance regime began in earnest during the 1990s and led to the establishment at the turn of the millennium of EU-level supervisory committees charged with setting general frameworks (Ferran 2012) which promoted the 'loose co-ordination' of member state activities at the European level while rule-making remained devolved with 'fully independent' national supervisors 'focusing essentially on national issues' (Merlin 2012: 13).

The reforms undertaken since beginning of the most recent financial crisis have been interpreted by some as consolidating financial governance at the regional level while reducing the scope and potential for experimentalism at particular points in time. Moloney (2010: 1320), for instance, has argued that the 'defining feature of the post-crisis reform movement seems to be the array of influences driving the regime toward greater centralization' in manners that place 'severe constraints . . . on local innovation and experimentation' (2010: 1382). Others have highlighted the legally binding rule making powers of the new European Supervisory Authorities (ESAs), emphasizing their enhanced capacity to overrule national supervisors and 'trump Member States' regulatory preferences' (Spendzharova 2012: 320).

Despite such centralization, rather than a single 'strong, pan-European financial "super-regulator"' (Perez 2010: 21), differences between the European Securities Markets Authority (ESMA), the European Banking Authority (EBA) and the European Insurance and Occupational Pensions Authority (EIOPA) continue to allow for variation in regulatory processes. Meanwhile, nuances in the legal and institutional structures of the three ESAs constrain the full centralization of authority at the regional level and have supported elements of EG in EU financial governance. For instance, through simple member state majorities national authorities are able to overturn EU-level decisions in appeals to the European Court of Justice. Moreover, sitting on the Board of Supervisors of each ESA, the heads of national supervisory institutions have the ability to act as a 'de facto brake' on ESA pronouncements (Ferran 2012: 68). While national actors can thus be regarded as the enduring 'center of gravity' in EU financial governance (Masciandaro *et al.* 2011: 213), the ongoing and varying involvement of the European Central Bank (ECB), the Commission, the European Parliament, the Council, and private associations in various aspects of rulemaking further contributes to an experimentalist regional governance structure (Schwarzer 2012).

Responses to ongoing financial instability further display experimentalism variation, such as with the Europeanization of insurance governance and the

Single Supervisory Mechanism to establish the EU-wide 'banking union'. Despite the centralization involved, these measures have been characterized by mixes of member state input, lack of permanently specified central powers and variations in the degrees of direct EU-level supervision for financial institutions of different sizes (Cœuré 2013; *Economist* 2012; Quaglia 2011, 2014).

The EU, experimentalism and global financial governance

How does EU EG interact with mechanisms of global financial governance? While a comprehensive analysis of the EU's engagement with all areas of global finance goes well beyond the scope of this contribution, an overview of a select set of interactions is useful for developing initial observations and providing directions for future research. We contrast the experimentalism of the IMF, a more traditional international setting, with the BCBS and the institutions of IFRS governance, which display significant experimentalist elements. As the BCBS is primarily public and the IFRS governance bodies are largely private, our comparison illustrates a further type of variation relevant to the character of global governance institutions. Together these organizations reflect a significant share of global financial regulatory activity.

Experimentalism at the IMF

The IMF is the most formal and bureaucratic of the institutions involved in the governance of global finance. It was designed primarily to manage monetary co-operation, especially with regard to exchange rates. As well, it manages large sums of money, including its lending to governments, which requires legal formal arrangements rather than informal commitments. Despite its nearly universal membership, the IMF system of quota and weighted voting has granted rule-making and executive staffing clout to industrialized Northern states (Woods 2006). The dominance of these states is associated with exercises of power politics, such as controlling the appointment of managing directors and favouring borrowing to countries where Northern banks are exposed to losses or with whom Northern governments are geo-strategically aligned (Copelovitch 2010).

In addition to its formal centralized structure and the influence of power politics in it, experimentalism is minimized at the IMF because of the character and agenda of its staff. The IMF has long been a highly insular organization (Momani 2005) strongly influenced by the neoclassical economic training of staff whom have marginalized factors exogenous to economic models, such as including local variation, in favour of 'one-size-fits-all' lending programmes (Woods 2006). Moreover, discussions in its Executive Board, which has been described as 'sterile' (Clegg 2012: 299), have exhibited little reflexivity.

Criticisms have led the IMF to implement some modest experimentalist reforms in recent years. Some 'mild forms' of learning over time have been highlighted (Chaudhary and Seabrooke 2009: 9; see also Broome and Seabrooke 2008) as the Fund has sought to integrate local variation through its Policy

Reduction Strategy Papers, which have required consultations with local stakeholders. Also with its Reports on Observance of Standards and Codes, the IMF has played a prominent role in reporting and evaluating rule implementation in its member states (Clegg and Moschella 2014). Finally, the Fund has attempted to construct mechanisms for evaluating its rule-making, most prominently with the 2001 creation of an Independent Evaluation Office (IEO). Yet, as the IEO staff originate from within the Fund, the potential of such evaluations have been limited (Weaver 2010).

Overall, the IMF continues to display a low capacity for learning and its rules have displayed little reflexive change over time (Jones 2013; Mody 2013). It remains relatively inhospitable to experimentalism, displaying instead the characteristics of traditional modes of global governance that involve blends of power politics with formal organization and law.

EU–IMF interactions

How has the EU performed in its engagement with the non-experimentalist IMF? Answering this question is complicated by the uncharacteristically close co-ordination between the IMF and the EU that has resulted from responses to the crises in Greece and other distressed EU member states. We return to this issue below after first providing a more general overview of the relatively ineffective EU engagement with the IMF.

EU interactions with the Fund have primarily been through key EU member states asserting their preferences individually or in quite traditional alliances. Consistent with the IMF's traditional character, the key EU powers, France, Germany and the United Kingdom have Executive Directors while the other EU member states are integrated into the constituency system (Hodson 2011: 102). Two committees seek to co-ordinate the EU role at the IMF: the Economic and Financial Committee's Subcommittee on the IMF (SCIMF), which operates out of Brussels; and the Washington-based EURIMF committee, which draws together EU-level actors such as the European Commission and the ECB. Neither committee operates in experimentalist mode and both are confined to co-ordinating more conventional bargaining on an *ad hoc* basis (Smaghi 2009).

There are no significant alternative mechanisms to allow the experimentalist features of the EU financial governance architecture to meaningfully interact with the IMF. The Fund's structure limits the ability to mobilize the non-traditional forms of power and influence (Hodson 2011: 97). EU institutions do not have formal representation on the Executive Board, and only the ECB holds observer status (Dur and Elsig 2011). Despite efforts to increase its prominence at the IMF during the financial crisis, the European Commission was 'all but invisible to the IMF Executive Board' (Hodson 2011: 110). European influence at the IMF can be transmitted through the European nationality of the Fund's managing director, which may reflect personal roots in European experiences, as may be evident in the distinctive qualities that Dominique Strauss-Kahn and Christine Lagarde have most recently exercised. Yet this cannot be a robust channel for the EU to exercise influence or derive benefits from the IMF, since the managing director's power is limited, and since this position is supposed to reflect the interests of the IMF membership as a whole.

The EU's more traditional interactions with the IMF over the past decade have been accompanied by a dwindling EU ability to engage with global financial governance through the IMF. This is because the G20 has gained influence at the expense of the IMF, and because discussion of reform at the IMF has focused on how to shift power away from the EU and United States of America (USA) towards countries such as Brazil, China and India. The G20 has gained influence in part because its more experimentalist character allowed it to adjust more quickly than the IMF to reflect the new centres of power in global finance (Woods 2010: 52). The rigidity and lack of experimentalism of IMF lending programmes also led countries that previously had borrowed from the IMF to resolve to avoid borrowing from the IMF again, which created serious difficulties for the IMF's identity and financing. While the global financial crisis that began in 2007 has temporarily reversed this decline, it is unlikely that the IMF will regain the utility it once had for promoting the interests of the EU and the USA in global finance.

Close EU–IMF collaboration in the recent EU member state crises is not inconsistent with this analysis. EU interactions with the Fund have remained non-experimental, involving specific financial considerations and 'one-size-fits' conditionality programmes for EU borrowers. The ability of the EU to direct more than two-thirds of the IMF's General Resources Account towards its own member states has been widely decried (Dettmer and Reiermann 2013; *EurActiv* 2013; Woods 2013). Moreover, borrowing from the IMF has not historically been seen as reflecting power, but instead as a clear sign of weakness. Beyond the ability to point to the IMF as external scapegoat for policy failures, it is difficult to treat as positive or beneficial the inclusion of the IMF in the 'Troika' that, along with the ECB and European Commission, has provided financial backing for distressed EU member states. Rather, the centring of these crises in Europe is consistent with the wider rebalancing of power in world politics that is the larger dynamic underlying EU–IMF interactions. Given the prominent role of the G20 since the beginning of the crisis, there is little reason to expect a reversal in the progressive shift in power away from the IMF to the G20 and other institutions where EU influence is diminished (Moschella 2012).

Our analysis now turns to EU interactions with two sets of institutions exhibiting more experimentalist elements than the IMF. The first, the BCBS, is more public, while the second, the set of IFRS governance bodies associated with the IASB, is more private.

Experimentalism at the BCBS

Founded in 1975 but with a charter formalized only in 2013, the BCBS has always exhibited elements of power politics in the development of its standards, which have been based on bargaining between major states that has excluded less powerful actors (Kapstein 1994; Wood 2005). Yet evidence of robust experimentalism at the BCBS can be seen in its informal organization and decision-making processes, as well as in its continual revision of banking standards in response to experience with their performance.

The problems that BCBS standards seek to address have the qualities that make temporal experimentalism across time more desirable than simultaneous experimentalism across jurisdictions. These standards aim to prevent jurisdictions from enacting excessively light regulations in order to attract financial flows. While it may be in the interest of any particular jurisdiction to offer light regulation, the effect on global systemic stability of all regulations being driven down by a 'race to the bottom' can be disastrous. For this reason the BCBS has increasingly sought to encourage uniformity in implementation by monitoring and reporting on compliance in order to reduce opportunities for experimentation across jurisdictions. This orientation against cross-jurisdictional experimentation should not be overstated, however, as the BCBS has also always permitted a degree of discretion in the national implementation of its standards.

Meanwhile, increased BCBS monitoring over time has added an experimentalist element that provides lessons that can be incorporated more systematically into future BCBS standards. From its founding, an important function of the BCBS has been to facilitate the sharing of lessons among regulators, which has expanded beyond its original 12 member states through consultative linkages with non-members, often organized in regional regulatory groupings, and by the expansion of the BCBS membership during the recent financial crisis to more closely match the G20's. The experimentalist character of the BCBS is exemplified by the three iterations of its most important banking standards: Basel I, II and III. Basel II sought to address the deficiencies of Basel I, as Basel III did for Basel II. Both Basel II and III were devised after extensive studies of alternatives and their likely effects, such as 'quantitative impact studies' where participating banks modelled the impact of proposed regulatory standards. For instance, one such study based on 2011 data involved 209 banks (Bank for International Settlements 2012). The most recent version of the standards was introduced in 2010 and involves a nine-year phase-in period, which allows for adjustments to be made, as well as for lessons to accumulate and guide a possible future set of Basel IV standards (KPMG 2013).

EU–BCBS interactions

The history of European interactions with the BCBS has tended to be obscured by the enthusiasm of American international political economy scholars for attributing global outcomes to United States (US) hegemonic power whilst ignoring the agency of other actors (e.g., Simmons 2001). For example Kapstein (1994) and others (Oatley and Nabors 1998) have attributed Basel I to co-ordinated threats to deny access to US markets. However, the definitive account of the history of the BCBS makes clear that the European Economic Community was heavily involved in shaping the content of Basel I, especially in the focus on risk ratios. For instance, BCBS member Huib Muller, who became BCBS Chair in 1989, made important contributions in the development of Basel I while chairing the EEC Banking Advisory Committee (Goodhart 2011: 158). Tarullo (2008: 40–1) confirms the important role of the EU at the beginning of discussions that led to Basel I:

> As a group, in fact, the European supervisors had leapt well ahead of their US, Canadian and Japanese counterparts in moving toward a risk-based standard for capital ratios . . . the trend towards convergence had been accelerated by the activities of the European Economic Community (EEC).

Tarullo goes on to note that 'the harmonization efforts of the Basel Committee and the European Community/Union have, in significant ways, reinforced one another ever since'.

Differences in the US and EU implementations of Basel III demonstrate the latter's more seamless integration with the key global banking regulatory response to the 2007–8 crisis. Basel III is being implemented in EU member states directly through the Capital Requirements Regulation, with national transposition through the Capital Requirement Directive IV. Despite notable member state conflict, for instance in the rejection of British, Spanish and Swedish preference to be able to impose higher standards (Howarth and Quaglia 2013), EU implementation of Basel III has been relatively smooth in comparison with the US enactment process. While the timeline for American implementation and the degree of non-compliance with specific Basel III requirements are similar to the EU's, a significant portion of US firms remain on a 'parallel run', where they continue to follow Basel I standards (Basel Committee on Banking Supervision 2013). Moreover, the US rules are entangled with the larger process of implementing the 2010 Dodd–Frank Wall Street Reform and Consumer Protection Act, which has been plagued by missed deadlines, court challenges and Congressional obstruction in the Republican-led House of Representatives. As of 1 November 2013, only 39.3 per cent of the 280 rule-making deadlines had passed with finalized rules, while merely 40.7 per cent of the total 398 rule-makings required had been finalized, with 28.9 per cent still not even proposed (Davis Polk 2013: 2). Meanwhile, the Volcker rule, which is at odds with global practices, has generated enormous controversy, and its overall fate remains uncertain (Lavelle 2014).

Overall, the implementation of global banking standards suggests that the EU is more closely linked and compatible with the Basel bank capital adequacy standards process than the US. In sharp contrast to the IMF, where the EU must rely on traditional diplomatic bargaining to promote its interests, the informality and continual revision of rule-making at the BCBS matches well with EU experimentalism. The close linkages between BCBS standards and EU enactment legislation further tie the two processes to one another. The embedding of Basel III implementation in well-established processes of EU experimentalist rule-making stands in contrast to the uncertain and conflictual reform paths exhibited in the US. Finally, the involvement of the EU and its member states in Basel standard-setting works against the conceptualization of this relationship as simple 'uploading' or 'downloading' of governance elements. Rather, integrating its rule-making within a global process allows EU to more effectively achieve regulatory policy objectives.

Experimentalism in IFRS governance

Significant experimentalist elements in the largely private sector governance of the IFRS complement the primarily public BCBS. The governance of global accounting standards is centred on the IASB, which was created in 2001 but built on the work of the International Accounting Standards Committee (IASC), which dates back to the 1970s. Today, the IFRS are used in over 120 jurisdictions worldwide, with the US being the most significant exception.

Power politics and formal structures have characterized certain aspects of IFRS governance. The initial creation of the IASB was marred by conflict between the two main powers in global finance, the US and the EU, over the structure of the organization. The US reliance on the expertise of industry professionals and large global accounting firms eventually triumphed in what represented a 'dramatic change' from the IASC (Richardson and Eberlein 2011: 226, see also Nölke 2011). This structure has led to a central role for individuals with backgrounds in the developed world financial sector and to criticism of a 'semi-open approach' (Botzem 2008) that has excluded a number of less powerful actors (Campbell-Verduyn 2014). Meanwhile, in response to the most recent financial crisis a public sector Monitoring Board was created to oversee the entire IFRS governance structure. Although there are expansion plans, the membership of the Board is confined to the European Commission as well as powerful American and Japanese public capital markets regulators, with only indirect representation of less powerful actors through the International Organization of Securities Commissions (IOSCO).

Like the BCBS standards, experimentation across jurisdictions is also constrained, because there is a high value in harmonizing implementation of the standards. A key function of accounting standards is to make corporate financial reporting clear to investors. The globalization of financial markets depends upon investors trusting that a valuation of one firm is comparable to a valuation of a different one. Creative accounting can be used to conceal problems.

Nevertheless, there are significant experimentalist elements in work associated with the IASB. While the IFRS contain enhanced levels of detail relative to earlier International Accounting Standards, the new standards remain broad principles relative to the more specific Generally Accepted Accounting Principles (GAAP) maintained by the US Financial Accounting Standards Board (FASB), which the IFRS are displacing as the primary standards used in international financial markets. The global accounting standards are non-binding principles whose decentralized implementation ultimately depends on their transposition into national and regional regulation. As such the global accounting standards are not always imposed wholesale, but have in a number of instances been more flexibly adopted into different national and regional 'dialects' (Véron 2012).

Additionally, the global accounting standards themselves are not static but 'living documents', revised in co-ordinated manners over time (Richardson and Eberlein 2011: 220). In this, the IFRS Interpretations Committee, which shares equal authority with the IASB, functions as a judiciary body clarifying the loosely defined global accounting standards through consultation with national and regional accounting standards boards. Both the IFRS Interpretations Committee and the IASB hold extensive public consultations, hearings and roundtable meetings while receiving guidance from the IFRS Advisory Council, a fourth IFRS governance body which is:

> comprised of a wide range of representatives from user groups, preparers, financial analysts, academics, auditors, regulators, professional accounting bodies and investor groups that are affected by and interested in the IASB's work. (IFRS 2012)

A further experimental feature of this structure is that the entire IFRS governance process is subject to revision through a formal public review process taking place every half-decade.

EU interactions with IFRS governance institutions

The EU has been closely integrated within the IFRS governance regime since the transformation of the IASC into the IASB at the turn of the millennium. Despite being on the losing end of the initial 'major confrontation' (Nölke 2011) with the US over the structure of the IASB, the EU nonetheless succeed in securing supermajority voting at the global accounting standard-setter. This voting structure has been important in avoiding the complete dominance of Anglo-Saxon perspectives at the IASB (Richardson and Eberlein 2011). Even more significantly, the 2002 EU regulation that led to the 2005 adoption of the IFRS for publicly traded companies contributed to the worldwide reversal away from what had until then been a trend towards the global adoption of the US GAAP. Although the attractiveness of American accounting standards had declined as a result of the massive Enron and WorldCom bankruptcies early in the new millennium, the EU delegation of accounting standard-setting authority to the IASB provided a major catalyst for the surge in worldwide adoption of the IFRS that very closely followed. The initial EU engagement with the newly created IASB thus contributed to the ascendancy of global as opposed to American accounting standards and has been interpreted as reflecting the growth of EU power relative to the US (Posner 2009, 2010).

As the most important jurisdiction using the IFRS, the EU benefits from its particularly important role in the feedback loops between the formulation of the accounting standards and their implementation, an important experimentalist aspect of IFRS governance. Extensive studies of comment letters have revealed the degree to which a range of EU actors have been amongst the most active participants involved in the public consultations of the IASB and the IFRS

Interpretations Committee (Larson 2007; Larson and Hertz 2013). The Union's endorsement process, meanwhile, involves a host of institutions mixing national standard-setters, member states, private sector associations and EU bodies to filter the global accounting standards and ensure their relevance, reliability, understandibility, comparability, as well as compatibility with the broader 'European public good' (de Bellis 2011: 270). Flexibility in the implementation of the IFRS and IAS permits the EU to not only match standards to suit its domestic purposes, but also to influence the global accounting standards themselves.

This process involves a mixture of experimentalist learning and power politics, since the integration of IASB and EU accounting allows the EU to expand its influence by threatening to not implement IASB standards. There are a number of examples of the way that the EU has exercised the leverage it enjoys from the integration of EU and IASB standards. Most prominently the 2005 EU 'hybrid' implementation of IAS 39 omitting certain sections on fair value standards for financial instruments led the IASB to amend and eliminate the controversial sections of that standard (Bengtsson 2011). Later, at the height of the recent financial crisis, the threat of the European Commission to 'take some unspecified action, which might lead to the IASB's losing its franchise to set accounting standards in the EU' pressured the global accounting body to partially loosen 'fair value' accounting standards, allowing financial institutions such as Deutsche Bank to declare mild pre-tax profits rather than hundred million euro losses (Zeff 2012: 829–30). Since then, the Economic and Financial Affairs Council (ECOFIN) has called for changes to fair value accounting to which the IASB responded through a number of concessions in the amending IAS 39 to IFRS 9 (Bengtsson 2011). Similar pressure was less noticeable but potentially underlying the timing of a report announcing that future members of the Monitoring Board would hail exclusively from jurisdictions adopting the IFRS (Jones 2012b), which was closely followed by the European Commission publicly questioning the American presence on the IASB, given US postponement of its decision to adopt the IFRS (Jones 2012a). Such strategies illustrate the extent to which the EU has become adept at benefiting from its integration with global accounting governance institutions.

Despite these benefits the EU has enjoyed from its integration with IFRS governance, and from the experimentalist elements in this integration, it is important to note that EU influence may decline as the IFRS has become 'nearly globally accepted' (Nölke 2011) and the IASB turns its attention towards the adoption and implementation of the IFRS in other regions of the world (Zeff 2012), which provides opportunities for other jurisdictions to increase their influence over the content of the standards at the expense of the EU. This may accelerate if the US continues to move closer to using IFRS. Intimations of this include the failure of the EU to secure a second seat at the newly established Monitoring Board (Bengtsson 2011), as well as to the leading role played by Americans on both sides of ongoing IASB–FASB convergence talks (de Bellis 2011).

Overall, the generation and application of the IFRS has involved quite dramatic institutional changes both at the EU and global levels. The EU's capacity to change and integrate itself into global governance arrangements with experimentalist elements has greatly increased the influence and benefits it enjoys with regard to the global accounting standards, as contrasted to alternatives such as continued reliance on US GAAP or the creation of more uniquely European standards controlled more directly by the EU.

As other actors also become more integrated into IFRS governance and EU influence has relatively declined, some scholars have echoed Mügge and Quaglia's emphasis on the importance for the EU of member state co-ordination and unity in global financial governance (e.g., Dewing and Russell 2008: 259). However, threats and requests issued by EU authorities in IFRS governance are likely only to carry weight to the extent that the EU is integrated in the process that links its practical uses of IFRS with the standard-setting process at the global level. As well, it is likely that the benefits that the EU has enjoyed so far from the experimentalist aspects of its engagement with IFRS governance institutions will continue to benefit the Union relative to competing jurisdictions in which experimentalism is weaker.

CONCLUSIONS

This contribution has argued that EG in the EU permits the 28-member Union to more fruitfully engage with an expanding number of global governance settings exhibiting experimentalist elements. This argument is contrary to the view that the lack of centralization and unity that comes with EG puts the EU at a disadvantage in a global setting dominated by unified centralized states engaged in power politics rather than experimentation. Against this, we have argued that EU EG is part of a larger epochal increase in experimentalism at all scales that signifies that the EU is increasingly likely to encounter and benefit from EG in global settings. At the same time more traditional features of world politics, such as power politics and formal organization and law, continue to persist alongside EG.

We have also argued that not all forms of experimentalism involve variations in implementation across jurisdictions or policy processes at particular points in time. In some areas of governance harmonized implementation is essential to the success of rules. Where it exists in such circumstances, experimentalism is likely to take place across time rather than across space or areas of policy.

The contribution assessed the empirical support for our claims by examining EU interactions with the IMF, the BCBS and the set of institutions governing the IFRS. The IMF displays the characteristics of traditional power politics and formal organization, with an insular staff. This organization was shown to exhibit little capacity for experimentalism, even with recent changes that have sought to respond to such criticisms. In contrast, despite the persistence of traditional elements of power politics and centralization, both the BCBS and IFRS governance bodies exhibit significant experimentalist features, including a capacity to change their standards in response to reflexive assessments of experiences with the implementation of standards in different locations and across time.

Consistent with our argument, the EU has been least successful in deriving benefits and exerting influence in its interactions with the IMF. The IMF's formal centralized structure and the insularity of its staff reduce the ability of experimentalist EU practices to effectively engage with the Fund. Instead, the EU is reliant upon the more conventional interactions of its leading member states in an environment where power is shifting away from the EU as the IMF loses influence to institutions like the G20 that better represent rising states, and where the change at the IMF itself also is oriented to increasing the role of those re-emerging powers. In this context, the closer EU–IMF co-operation that has arisen in responding to recent EU member state sovereign debt crises can hardly be seen as positive for the influence of the Union in global financial governance.

Also consistent with our argument, the EU has engaged more effectively with the more experimental BCBS and IFRS governance bodies. In both cases, experimentalism has assisted the EU in coping with the changes these global governance institutions are experiencing and in interacting with the detail of their standards as they are developed. This differs from the notion of policy 'uploading' and 'downloading' to and from the global level, which implies that these bodies are simply transit points rather than collective processes solving collective problems. Yet integration with these processes does also increase the exposure of EU policy to influences from elsewhere, especially from the US in the case of IFRS governance. As other countries become more integrated with these processes, EU influence is likely to continue to decline.

However, we do not believe that the EU would benefit from acting more like a conventional centralized unified state in a global financial system in which inter-state power is becoming dispersed and multi-polar. Instead, drawing on its distinctive capacity for experimentalism is most likely to maximize the capacity of the EU to influence global processes, especially in complex areas requiring the generation of new knowledge and governance mechanisms. Our view, therefore, is that it would weaken the EU to abandon EG in favour of a unified command and control mode of governance, even in settings where traditional power politics persist.

Finally, there are important caveats to these findings that must be acknowledged. First, there clearly remain further sets of factors relevant to our argument, including, for example, the geographic remove that makes the IMF headquarters in the American capital more physically distant from EU influence than the BCBS in Switzerland and the IASB in London. Second, it is difficult to draw wide generalizations from this relatively brief overview of a small number of cases. To strengthen our conclusions further research investigating EU interactions with other global financial governance institutions, such as the IOSCO, is therefore required. However, we believe that this contribution has highlighted sufficient initial evidence that EG enhances EU influence in global financial governance to merit further exploration of these relationships.

Biographical notes: Malcolm Campbell-Verduyn is a PhD candidate in the Department of Political Science at McMaster University, Ontario, Canada. Tony Porter is professor of political science at McMaster University, Ontario, Canada.

ACKNOWLEDGEMENTS

We thank Daniel Mügge for organizing this collection, as well as the EU in Global Finance workshop held at the University of Amsterdam in February 2013. We acknowledge funding from the Social Science and Humanities Research Council of Canada, grant #410-11-2376. For valuable comments on earlier drafts of this contribution we thank the other workshop participants, as well as two referees. Any omissions or errors remain our own.

REFERENCES

Abbott, K. and Snidal, D. (2001) 'International "standards" and international governance', *Journal of European Public Policy* 8(3): 345–70.

Bank for International Settlements (2012) 'Quantitative impact study results published by the Basel Committee', Press release, 20 September, available at http://www.bis.org/press/p120920.htm (accessed 9 November 2013).

Basel Committee on Banking Supervision (2013) 'Report to G20 finance ministers and central bank governors on monitoring implementation of Basel III regulatory refo', Bank for International Settlements, available at http://www.bis.org/publ/bcbs249.pdf (accessed 27 April 2013).

Beck, U., Giddens, A. and Lash, S. (1994) *Reflexive Modernization: Politics, Tradition and Aesthetics in the Modern Social Order*, Stanford, CA: Stanford University Press.

Bengtsson, E. (2011) 'Repoliticalization of accounting standard setting – the IASB, the EU and the global financial crisis', *Critical Perspectives on Accounting* 22(6): 567–80.

Botzem, S. (2008) 'Transnational expert-driven standardisation: accountancy governance from a professional point of view', in J.-C. Graz and A. Nölke (eds), *Transnational Private Governance and its Limits*, London and New York: Routledge, pp. 44–57.

Börzel, T. (2012) 'Experimentalism in the EU: the emperor's new clothes?', *Regulation and Governance* 6(3): 378–84.

Brassett, J., Richardson, B. and Smith, W. (2012) 'Private experiments in global governance: primary commodity roundtables and the politics of deliberation', *International Theory* 4(3): 367–99.

Broome, A. and Seabrooke, L. (2008) 'The IMF and experimentalist governance in small Western states', *The Round Table: The Commonwealth Journal of International Affairs* 97(395): 205–26.

Campbell-Verduyn, M. (2014). 'Conflicting trends and tensions in post-crisis reforms of transnational accounting standards', in T. Porter (ed.), *Transnational Financial Regulation after the Crisis*, London: Routledge.
Chaudhary, S. and Seabrooke, L. (2009) 'Pragmatic numbers: how the IMF creates policy dialogue for financial reform', *CSGR Working Paper 261/09*, Coventry: Centre for the Study of Globalisation and Regionalisation, Department of Politics and International Studies, University of Warwick.
Clegg, L. (2012) 'Global governance behind closed doors: the IMF boardroom, the Enhanced Structural Adjustment Facility, and the intersection of material power and norm stabilisation in global politics', *Review of International Organization* 7: 285–308.
Clegg, L. and Moschella, M. (2014) 'The managers of information: international organizations, data, and financial stability', in T. Porter (ed.), *Transnational Financial Regulation after the Crisis*, London: Routledge.
Cœuré, B. (2013) 'Central banking: where are we headed?', Speech to Institute for Monetary and Financial Stability, Goethe University, Frankfurt, 7 February 2013, available at http://www.ecb.int/press/key/date/2013/html/sp130207.en.html (accessed 28 April 2013).
Copelovitch, M. (2010) 'Master or servant? Common agency and the political economy of IMF lending', *International Studies Quarterly* 54: 49–77.
Davis Polk (2013) 'Dodd–Frank progress report', available at http://www.davispolk.com/sites/default/files/Nov2013_Dodd.Frank_.Progress.Report_0.pdf (accessed 13 November 2013).
de Bellis, M. (2011) 'EU and global private regulatory regimes: the accounting and auditing sectors', in E. Chiti and B. Mattarella (eds), *Global Administrative Law and EU Administrative Law Relationships, Legal Issues and Comparison*, Berlin and Heidelberg: Springer-Verlag, pp. 269–92.
De Búrca, G., Keohane, R. and Sabel, C. (2013) 'New modes of pluralist global governance', *New York University Journal of International Law and Politics* 45 (3): 723–86.
Dettmer, M. and Reiermann, C. (2013) 'IMF board attacks euro crisis management', *Der Spiegel International*, 6 March.
Dewing, I. and Russell, P. (2008) 'Financial integration in the EU: the first phase of EU endorsement of International Accounting Standards', *Journal of Common Market Studies* 46 (2): 243–64.
Dur, A. and Elsig, M. (2011) 'Principals, agents, and the European Union's foreign economic policies', *Journal of European Public Policy* 18(3): 323–38.
Economist (2012) 'Made in Brussels', 17 November.
Euractiv (2013) 'Brazilian refuses to back fresh IMF aid for Greece', 1 August.
Ferran, E. (2012) ' Crisis-driven regulatory reform: where in the world is the EU going?', in E. Ferran, N. Moloney, J. Hill and J. Coffee Jr. (eds), *The Regulatory Aftermath of the Global Financial Crisis*, Cambridge: Cambridge University Press, pp. 1–89.
Giddens, A. (1990) *The Consequences of Modernity*, Stanford, CA: Stanford University Press.
Goodhart, C. (2011) *The Basel Committee on Banking Supervision: A History of the Early Years, 1974–1997*, Cambridge: Cambridge University Press.
Haas, E. (1990) *When Knowledge is Power: Three Models of Change in International Organizations*, Berkeley, CA: University of California Press.
Haas, P. and Haas, E. (1995) 'Learning to learn: improving international governance', *Global Governance* 1(3): 255–84.
Hodson, D. (2011) *Governing the Euro Area in Good Times and Bad*, Oxford: Oxford University Press.

Howarth, D. and Quaglia, L. (2013) 'Banking on stability: the political economy of new capital requirements in the European Union', *Journal of European Integration* 35: 333–46.

IFRS (2012) 'IFRS Advisory Council membership', available at http://www.ifrs.org/The+organisation/Advisory+bodies/IFRS+Advisory+Council/IFRS+Advisory+Council+membership/IFRS+Advisory+Council+membership.htm (accessed 7 March 2012).

Jones, C. (2013). 'IMF's history of self-flagellation suggests it seldom learns', *Financial Times*, 7 June.

Jones, H. (2012a) 'EU queries US seat on global accounting body', *Reuters*, 18 July.

Jones, H. (2012b) 'Global accounting reform ups pressure on US to sign up', *Reuters*, 9 February.

Jørgensen, K. (2009) 'The European Union and international organizations: a framework for analysis', in K. Jørgensen (ed.), *The European Union and International Organizations*, New York: Routledge, pp. 1–20.

Kapstein, E. (1994) *Governing the Global Economy: International Finance and the State*, Cambridge, MA: Harvard University Press.

Kissack, R. (2010) *Pursuing Effective Multilateralism: The European Union, International Organisations and the Politics of Decision Making*, New York: Palgrave Macmillan.

KPMG (2013) 'Basel 4 – emerging from the mist?', available at http://www.kpmg.com/Global/en/IssuesAndInsights/ArticlesPublications/regulatory-challenges/Documents/emerging-from-the-mist.pdf (accessed 10 November 2013).

Larson, R. (2007) 'Constituent participation and the IASB's International Financial Reporting Interpretations Committee', *Accounting in Europe* 4(2): 207–54.

Larson, R. and Herz, P. (2013) 'A multi-issue/multi-period analysis of the geographic diversity of IASB comment letter participation', *Accounting in Europe* 10(1): 99–151.

Lavelle, K. (2014) 'Implementing the Volcker Rule in national and international politics', in T. Porter (ed.), *Transnational Financial Regulation after the Crisis*, London: Routledge.

Masciandaro, D., Nieto, M. and Quintyn, M. (2011) 'Exploring governance of the new European Banking Authority – a case for harmonization?', *Journal of Financial Stability* 7(4): 204–14.

Merlin, M. (2012) 'Financial supervision in Europe after the crisis', in M. Balling, F. Lierman, F. Van den Spiegel, R. Ayadi and D. Llewellyn (eds), *New Paradigm in Banking, Financial Markets and Regulation?*, Vienna: SUERF, pp. 13–18.

Mody, A. (2013) 'Misreading the global economy', *Project Syndicate*, 23 May.

Moloney, N. (2010) 'EU financial market regulation after the global financial crisis: "more Europe" or more risks?', *Common Market Law Review* 47: 1317–83.

Momani, B. (2005) 'Recruiting and diversifying IMF technocrats,' *Global Society* 19(2): 167–87.

Moschella, M. (2012) 'IMF surveillance in crisis: the past, present and future of the reform process', *Global Society* 26(1): 43–60.

Mügge, D. (2011) 'The European presence in global financial governance: a principal–agent perspective', *Journal of European Public Policy* 18(3): 383–402.

Mügge, D. (ed). (forthcoming) *Europe and the Governance of Global Finance*, Oxford: Oxford University Press.

Nance, M. and Cottrell, M. (2013) 'A turn toward experimentalism? Rethinking security and governance in the twenty-first century', *Review of International Studies*. doi:10.1017/S026021051300017X

Newman, A. and Bach, D. (2014) 'The European Union as hardening agent: soft law and the diffusion of global financial regulation', *Journal of European Public Policy* 20(30), doi: 10.1080/13501763.2014.882968.

Nölke, A. (2011) 'International Accounting Standards Board', in T. Hale and D. Held (eds), *Handbook of Transnational Governance Institutions and Innovations*, Cambridge: Polity, pp. 66–70.
Oatley, T, and Nabors, R. (1998) 'Redistributive cooperation: market failure, wealth transfers, and the Basle Accord', *International Organization* 52(1): 35–54.
Overdevest, C. and Zeitlin, J. (2012) 'Assembling an experimentalist regime: transnational governance interactions in the forest sector', *Regulation and Governance*, doi: 10.1111/j.1748-5991.2012.01133.x.
Perez, S. (2010) 'Financial regulation in Europe: divergent institutional responses in the ages of globalization and an untidy compromise', *Perspectives on Europe* 40(2): 20–6.
Porter, T. (ed.) (2014) *Transnational Financial Regulation after the Crisis*, London: Routledge.
Posner, E. (2009) 'Making rules for global finance: transnational regulatory cooperation at the turn of the millennium,' *International Organization* 63(4): 665–99.
Posner, E. (2010) 'Sequence as explanation: the international politics of accounting standards', *Review of International Political Economy* 17(4): 639–64.
Posner, E. (n.d.) 'An experimentalist turn in international financial regulatory cooperation?', in J. Zeitlin, (ed.), *Extending Experimentalist Governance? The European Union and Transnational Regulation*, manuscript in preparation.
Quaglia, L. (2011) 'The politics of insurance regulation and supervision reform in the European Union', *Comparative European Politics* 9(1): 100–22.
Quaglia, L. (2013) 'The European Union, the USA and international standard setting by regulatory fora in finance', *New Political Economy*, doi: 10.1080/13563467.2013.796449.
Quaglia, L. (2014) 'The sources of European Union influence in international financial regulatory fora', *Journal of European Public Policy* 21(3), doi: 10.1080/13501763.2014.882970.
Richardson, A, and Eberlein, B. (2011) 'Legitimating transnational standard-setting: the case of the international accounting standards board', *Journal of Business Ethics* 98(2): 217–45.
Sabel, C. and Zeitlin, J. (2008) 'Learning from difference: the new architecture of experimentalist governance in the EU', *European Law Journal* 14(3): 271–27.
Sabel, C. and Zeitlin, J. (eds) (2010a) *Experimentalist Governance in the European Union: Towards a New Architecture*, Oxford: Oxford University Press.
Sabel, C. and Zeitlin, J. (2010b) 'Learning from difference: the new architecture of experimentalist governance in the EU', in C. Sabel and J. Zeitlin, (eds), *Experimentalist Governance in the European Union: Towards a New Architecture*, Oxford: Oxford University Press, pp. 1–28.
Sabel, C. and Zeitlin, J. (2011) 'Experimentalist governance', in D. Levi-Faur (ed.), *The Oxford Handbook of Governance*, Oxford University Press, pp. 169–83.
Schwarzer, D. (2012) 'The euro area crises, shifting power relations and institutional change in the European Union', *Global Policy* 3: 28–41.
Simmons, B. (2001) 'The international politics of harmonization: the case of capital market regulation', *International Organization* 55(3): 589–620.
Smaghi, L. (2009) 'A single EU seat in the International Monetary Fund?', in K. Jørgensen, (ed.), *The European Union and International Organizations*, Abingdon: Routledge, pp. 61–79.
Spendzharova, A. (2012) 'Is more Brussels the solution? New European Union member states' preferences about the European financial architecture', *Journal of Common Market Studies* 50(2): 315–34.
Tarullo, D. (2008) *Banking on Basel: The Future of International Financial Regulation*, Washington, DC: Peterson Institute for International Economics.

Véron, N. (2012) 'Financial reform after the crisis: an early assessment', in B. Eichengreen and B. Park (eds), *The Global Economy After the Financial Crisis.* Singapore: World Scientific Publishing, pp. 7–26.
Weaver, C. (2010). 'The politics of performance evaluation: independent evaluation at the International Monetary Fund', *The Review of International Organizations,* 5(3): 365–85.
Wood, D. (2005) *Governing Global Banking: The Basel Committee and the Politics of Financial Globalization,* Burlington, VT: Ashgate.
Woods, N. (2006) *The Globalizers: the IMF, the World Bank and their Borrowers,* New York: Cornell University Press.
Woods, N. (2010) 'Global governance after the financial crisis: a new multilateralism or the last gasp of the great powers?', *Global Policy* 1(1): 51–63.
Woods, N. (2013) 'Global institutions after the Crisis', *Project Syndicate,* 6 September.
Zeff, S. (2012) 'The Evolution of the IASC into the IASB, and the challenges it faces', *The Accounting Review* 87(3): 807–37.

The European Union as hardening agent: soft law and the diffusion of global financial regulation

Abraham Newman and David Bach

ABSTRACT Soft law promulgated by transnational networks is one of the hallmarks of governance in global finance. Standard accounts alternatively view such governance as a fast and flexible solution to transnational problems or weakly institutionalized club standards epiphenomenal to great power interests. We argue that dominant perspectives' view of soft law is misguided, as soft law in global finance cannot be understood in isolation from domestic law. Viewing soft law through the prism of multilevel governance highlights the role European integration in particular plays in 'hardening' soft law provisions, thereby shaping the global diffusion of such standards. As soft law becomes embedded in domestic law, its certainty and durability are enhanced while at the same time its flexibility is reduced. Case studies of the diffusion of international accounting standards and close-out netting rules for over-the-counter derivatives provide empirical support for the importance of domestic law in the global diffusion of soft law.

The global regulation of finance is marked by its reliance on soft law rules promulgated by non-treaty-based networks (Brummer 2011; Zaring 1998). Fairly informal bodies, such as the Basel Committee for Banking Supervision or the International Accounting Standards Board, shape market competition through capital adequacy rules, accounting standards, and other technical and substantive rules (Alexander *et al.* 2006; Davies and Green 2008; Oatley and Nabors 1998; Porter 2005a; Tarullo 2008). On the one hand, such standards have been championed as a new fast and flexible solution to transnational financial governance (Slaughter 2004; Zaring 1998). On the other hand, power-based theories have characterized them as epiphenomenal to great power interests with limited application to politically charged issues (Drezner 2007).

We argue that dominant perspectives' view of the role of soft law in global finance is misguided, as soft law in global finance cannot be understood in isolation from domestic law. We advocate viewing the role of soft law through the prism of multilevel governance and argue that European integration in particular promotes soft law diffusion (Hooghe and Marks 2003). Across multiple issues in global finance, the European Union (EU) acts as a legalization mechanism that transforms soft law from informal transnational best practice into embedded rules backed by domestic law (Caporaso and Tarrow 2009; Goldstein *et al.* 2000).

The decision by the EU, or a significant number of member states, to adopt and incorporate such standards into law alters global diffusion dynamics. Once the EU, or a significant number of member states, have legally committed to a set of soft law standards, these standards are no longer simply informal institutions or instances of private global governance. Rather, they have been 'hardened' and are henceforth backed by domestic law. Such hardening alters the incentives of EU actors to support and promote the global regime. At the same time, it alters the attractiveness of the regime to other jurisdictions. This is because European commitment frequently constitutes a tipping point, signaling to other jurisdictions that a proposed private standard will likely diffuse widely. While national or regional regulatory incorporation boosts certainty in the private regime, the traditional flexibility ascribed to such regimes is reduced, as they become entangled in the domestic regulatory, legislative and legal structures of large markets (Shaffer and Pollack 2009). By incorporating analytically the role of domestic law, our approach leads us to question the flexibility of such standards emphasized in both the private actor governance and power-based approaches. At the same time, it suggests much more predictability and durability. This contribution, then, focuses on the way the EU – advertently and at times inadvertently – transforms and institutionalizes informal voluntary best practices into domestically embedded legal rules, thereby shaping global diffusion dynamics.

To demonstrate the way in which the EU acts as a hardening agent for international soft law, we examine two critical cases of global financial governance: international accounting standards and close-out netting rules for over-the-counter derivatives. Accounting standards is often held up as a prime example of private transnational governance. While the important role of private actors in shaping global standards is undeniable, we show how EU endorsement of international financial reporting standards (IFRS) and their embedding within EU law gave private efforts a tremendous boost and transformed a mere voluntary standards project into the kernel of global regulation. The derivatives case takes the argument a step further by demonstrating the important role that national legislatures continue to play and highlights how ongoing EU-led financial re-regulation efforts create an opportunity structure for transnational policy entrepreneurs. Taken together, the cases offer the empirical context for a robust plausibility probe that explores the effect of soft law hardening via supranational imposition and national embedding for global diffusion.

The contribution makes several important contributions to the literature on the EU's role in global governance. It couples two dynamics that increasingly receive attention in research on international regulation and yet have been discussed largely separately: the EU as a global regulatory actor and the rise of international soft law in finance (Bach and Newman 2007; Brummer 2011; Büthe and Mattli 2011; Mügge 2011; Posner 2009a; Underhill and Zhang 2008). Moreover, it highlights the links between domestic rules and global standards, broadening the discussion of soft law and private governance (Bach and Newman 2010; Helleiner and Pagliari 2011; Kaczmarek and Newman 2011; Putnam 2009). Finally, it helps resolve an important empirical puzzle concerning the widespread use of soft law: the remarkable resilience of many international soft law standards despite their demonstrably shallow institutionalization at the global level.

SOFT LAW IN GLOBAL FINANCIAL REGULATION: MORE THAN SECOND BEST?

The global regulation of finance relies on a patchwork of informal regulatory networks comprised of public and private actors. Bodies such as the International Organization of Securities Commissions (IOSCO), the Basel Committee on Banking Regulation, the International Association of Insurance Supervisor (IAIS), the International Accounting Standards Board (IASB), and the International Derivatives and Swaps Association (IDSA) promulgate best practices and standards (Alexander *et al.* 2006; Davies and Green 2008; Underhill and Zhang 2008). This soft law regime is striking in its thin degree of institutionalization and widespread reliance on voluntary compliance (Brummer 2011; Porter 2005a).[1] Nevertheless, such soft law standards have diffused widely and are shaping market dynamics. What explains the adoption of standards promulgated by such informal institutions is one of the critical questions in current research on global governance.

Extant research in the institutionalist tradition commonly explains these bodies' influence by focusing on the interaction of technical knowledge held by private actors and the disciplining effects of the market. According to these studies, private actors with deep sector expertise enjoy broad legitimacy to shape transnational rules and market participants largely adopt these standards because of competitive pressures (Büthe and Mattli 2011; Mattli and Büthe 2005; Perry and Nolke 2006).

An alternative, power-based literature offers a very different perspective on the spread of network-based standards. Viewing such standards as club goods, authors in this tradition argue that their adoption by large and powerful markets create trading up pressure (Drezner 2007; Posner 2009a; Simmons 2001). If the United States (US) and EU have adopted a particular capital adequacy standard, for example, banks that fall below it risk exclusion from those markets, as well as the reputational cost of failing to comply with 'best practice' (Kapstein 1992; Oatley and Nabors 1998).

These perspectives explicitly or implicitly take to heart the pervasive view of soft law as under-institutionalized (Abbott and Snidal 2000; Kahler and Lake 2009; Vabulas and Snidal 2013). Without treaty-based organizations to guarantee compliance and implementation, advocates of private actor governance must invoke market discipline to explain soft law adoption, while those viewing soft law primarily as club standards invoke the whims of great powers for their causal constructs. In short, according to these perspectives, soft law represents a regulatory 'second best' that lacks the credible commitment needed in international co-operation. While soft law may serve as a fast and flexible response to co-ordination problems when there are few distributional or enforcement problems, conventional wisdom holds that it faces the pernicious challenge of shirking or cherry-picking. Owing to its lack of legalization, in which case legal actors and institutions would create pressure for convergence, soft law is characterized by considerable uncertainty (Goldstein *et al.* 2000; Shaffer and Pollack 2009). This uncertainty, in turn, should undermine the spread and diffusion of such rules.

In addition, the analytic attention on private actors or powerful states has produced a series of narrow 'setting standards'-debates that has focused on who exerts the most influence over agendas (Bach and Newman 2007; Mügge 2011; Perry and Nolke 2006; Posner 2009a; Quaglia 2014; Underhill and Zhang 2008). While such distributional trade-offs are important, not enough attention has been paid to how transnationally promulgated rules spread and why some reach critical mass of adopters and others do not. We believe that the scholarly debate has largely missed fundamental changes in the institutionalization of the global regime for finance that condition diffusion processes, specifically the way soft law standards are hardened through domestic law in leading jurisdictions.

To broaden the debate, we propose to place soft law dynamics within a multilevel governance framework in which these informal rules interact and are embedded within regional and national law. Owing to disciplinary boundaries within political science, international and domestic law are often kept separate, with International Relations (IR) scholars focusing primarily on treaty-based international law (Dunoff and Pollack 2012; Helleiner and Pagliari 2011). This silo approach hinders the tracing of causal processes across levels and domains. There are, of course, exceptions. Work on extraterritoriality and diffusion, for example, demonstrates the important and growing interdependencies of domestic law in global governance (Bach and Newman 2010; Kaczmarek and Newman 2011; Powell and Staton 2009; Putnam 2009; Raustiala 2002; Simmons and Elkins 2004; Zaring 2004).

In this contribution, we show not just how international soft law best practices become legally binding, domestically embedded rules (Eberlein and Newman 2008; Lavelle 2011; Singer 2007), but also the consequence of this legal incorporation for global governance. While such embedding by early adopters is a key step in the diffusion process, particularly if they are leading jurisdictions such as the US or EU, there is an important trade-off confronting the underlying soft law-promulgating bodies. First, domestic politics in early adopters will slow the speed of standards change in those jurisdictions. Second, powerful jurisdictions will seek to engage the governance of the private regime according to their preferences. As a result, once a set of private standards has been formally embedded domestically, it may become less flexible and amendable to change at the international level. Post-embedding, expert-driven agenda-setting must now confront the political realities of the domestic regulatory setting in leading jurisdictions (Barr and Miller 2006; Zaring 2004). Stakeholders become invested in the standard as regulators develop local rules to interpret and implement them. Similarly, even the most powerful jurisdictions cannot simply ignore their prior commitment to a nominally voluntary standard as domestic veto points and regulatory politics keep said commitment in check (Goldstein *et al.* 2000). As transnational soft law becomes embedded within national law, it is no longer epiphenomenal to state power or technical experts. In terms of institutionalization, after domestic embedding, the initially informal soft law standards enjoy much of the domestic certainty of ratified 'treaty-based' rules held up in existing literature as the non-plus-ultra of global governance (Goldstein *et al.* 2000).

When such domestic embedding occurs in leading markets, it has global spillover effects, which can alter the character of the global regulatory regime and promote adoption in other markets. First and most obvious, early adopters have every reason to proselytize their chosen soft law standard within cross-border expert networks in a traditional agenda-shaping fashion. This is because once a leading market has formally committed to a set of soft law standards, its regulators have an incentive to promote these rules to mitigate regulatory adjustment costs or competitive disadvantages for their firms. Failure to do so risks inefficient regulatory fragmentation if other leading markets choose competing rules or, even worse, costly lock-in (Büthe and Mattli 2011). To ward off standards fragmentation and Pareto-inefficient lock-in, leading domestic regulators frequently go beyond merely praising the merit of their adopted solution. They rely on extraterritorial provisions in domestic law to impose local rules on foreign firms (Farrell 2003; Kaczmarek and Newman 2011; Newman 2008). It is not simply the epiphenomenal decision by powerful states that alters the diffusion process, but, ironically, the binding nature of domestic law within them that spurs the global promotion of such rules. To put it another way, domestic law offers large markets the regulatory capacity necessary to enforce and promote the standard (Bach and Newman 2007; Newman 2008).

Equally important, the incorporation of informal rules and standards into the domestic law of large markets mitigates the uncertainty that frequently besets international soft law provisions (Shaffer and Pollack 2009). Domestic embedding is a credible and costly commitment that signals the viability of the standard to other jurisdictions. Once such standards become domestic rules and are subject to domestic veto points, typical domestic political dynamics kick in, which reduce the likelihood of sudden policy shift. To remain effective, transnational standard-setters must engage regulators from leading markets that have adopted their promulgated rules and create mechanism to incorporate their concerns. A mutual dependence emerges between the standard-setter and leading adopters (Richardson and Eberlein 2011). This prevents rapid or radical changes to the transnational standard, since transnational standard-setters know they cannot advance too far ahead of powerful domestic regulators or risk losing influence. The mutual dependence sends a costly signal to other jurisdictions regarding the predictability of the soft law regime.

We are particularly interested in the ways in which the EU has transformed the character of soft law in global finance and thereby promoted its adoption globally. The EU, however, is not the only hardening agent for international soft law. A potent example of the US giving a private sector solution global reach by formally embedding it domestically is the regime for Internet domain names (Bach 2010). Nevertheless, there are several reasons why the EU is particularly important to the embedding of international soft law in finance. The single market project, along with financial market integration and the EU response to the financial and sovereign debt crisis, has produced nearly two decades of constant legislating in the financial domain (Posner 2009b; Quaglia 2010). Moreover, the 'better regulation' project instituted a series of ongoing regulatory reviews and directive reforms, which further guarantee the routine reconsideration of regional rules of finance (Sabel and Zeitlin 2010).

Given this massive and institutionalized re-regulation process, the EU creates a significant opportunity structure for the embedding of global soft law standards within a multilevel governance process (Borzel and Risse 2000; Joachim 2003). This occurs in two principle ways. On the one hand, soft law can enter directly into EU law from the top down. We call this 'supranational imposition'. Increasingly. EU directives make direct reference to international soft law standards. For example, the Banking Directive and Capital Adequacy Directive of 2006 incorporate Basel II specifications.[2] As a result, all member states embedded this soft law reform promulgated by the non-treaty-based Basel Committee into their domestic law, just as it became legally binding at the supranational level. On the other hand, even in cases when the EU does not directly mandate the incorporation of specific soft law standards, the re-regulation process of Europe's financial markets repeatedly opens up the national legislative processes to transnational soft law entrepreneurs. EU directives 'unfreeze' the domestic regulatory agenda across a large number of countries by requiring implementing legislation (Borzel and Risse 2000; Posner 2009b; Weir and Skocpol 1985). As national parliaments consider such implementing legislation, lobby groups can press for the embedding of soft law rules and do so simultaneously, and with similar arguments, across almost 30 jurisdictions (Featherstone and Radaelli 2003). European integration creates an opportunity structure for transnational policy entrepreneurs to promote legislative change within member states. We call this second pathway 'national embedding'.

We expect that the pathway through which embedding happens to affect the diffusion of rules globally. Regardless of pathway, European domestic legal incorporation boosts the predictability of a soft law regime, which should spur adoption. Beyond that, however, differences emerge. First, in instances of supranational imposition, we expect EU officials to promote the adoption of the soft law standard far more actively than in cases of domestic embedding. The reason is that EU officials, in the former case, have a more direct stake in the soft law standard, want to avoid global fragmentation, and can leverage extraterritorial provisions of EU law. In national embedding, any active promotion largely bypasses EU officials and extraterritorial provisions, such as restricting market access to non-compliant foreign firms, occurs at the member state level only. Instead, national embedding provides legitimacy to transnational entrepreneurs as they attempt to promote their standard globally. Rapid adoption across member states allows entrepreneurs to invoke peer pressure, providing potential adopters with both a proof of concept and evidence that the standard will avoid fragmentation. Second, we expect that collective action problems would reduce a group of member states' ability to shape transnational standard evolution in national embedding, at least when compared to supranational imposition. Finally, whereas supranational imposition legitimizes and empowers a single soft law focal point for a domestic market of more than 500 million people, national embedding entails the possibility of slightly varying domestic adoption schemes, thereby leading to more of a 'focal zone' than a specific focal point. In sum, we expect accelerated global diffusion as a result of EU hardening regardless of pathway, but for diffusion patterns to vary by pathway.

In the following section, we examine two cases of international soft law in finance: accounting and close-out netting standards. Prior research on international accounting standards has produced two competing views, with one set of authors claiming the rise of the International Accounting Standards Board (IASB) is an instance of private actor global governance and others finding evidence for the club standards perspective by highlighting US and EU efforts to exert influence over IASB. Our goal is not to adjudicate between these competing views. Rather, it is to highlight the broader role of the EU in transforming global accounting standards from a voluntary regime based exclusively on soft law to an embedded and institutionalized set of rules backed by domestic and EU law. Our second case examines close-out netting standards for over-the-counter derivatives. Here, we explore the second pathway – national embedding.

DIFFUSION OF INTERNATIONAL ACCOUNTING STANDARDS THROUGH SUPRANATIONAL IMPOSITION

The international regulation of accounting standards often strikes outsiders as highly technical and arcane. Behind the complexities, however, sit the basic operating system of the global economy (Büthe and Mattli 2011; Veron 2007). Indeed, the stakes could not be higher – weak standards facilitate fraud and risk systemic stability as scandals such as the collapse of Enron or the securitization of debt in the 2008 financial crisis demonstrate (Eaton 2005).

Over time, diverse national accounting systems and standards have emerged across jurisdictions, each firmly rooted in its respective political economy. Not surprisingly, national rules tend to favor specific economic constituencies and support distinct styles of capitalism, privileging patient capital or shareholder interests (Botzem and Quack 2009; Nölke and Perry 2008). It is equally evident that divergent accounting standards across major markets generate inefficiencies and costs. By obstructing price discovery and hindering cross-border investments, they promote an inefficient allocation of capital and increase financing costs. Functional demand for harmonization is therefore logical. However, any such efforts carry substantial political risks because of the distributional implications identified above.

The path to global accounting harmonization has been shaped by these factors and has been anything but a straight line (Botzem 2012). From the 1970s to the early 2000s, little progress towards common global rules was made. In one forum after the next, competing interests stymied reform. Then, suddenly, in a matter of a decade, thousands of firms from Asia, Australia, Europe and the Americas began using International Financial Reporting Standards (IFRS) developed by the International Accounting Standards Board (IASB).[3]

Much of the existing literature focuses on the relative influence of different actors in shaping the content of IFRS. Power-based accounts such as Simmons (2001) or Posner (2010) explore the relative influence of the US and EU. Those emphasizing private actor governance stress the role of the epistemic community underpinning IASB (Perry and Nölke 2005; Porter 2005b). Finally, institutionalists such as Büthe and Mattli (2011) stress the institutional fit between domestic private sector organizations and the IASB.

Clearly, major powers as well as technical experts have shaped the content of IASB standards. A missing piece in existing accounts is the way in which EU involvement has transformed the character of the IFRS regime from a set of voluntary best practices to a highly institutionalized set of global rules. With the decision of the European Commission in 2002 to endorse IASB standards for European firms listed on qualifying exchanges, the EU embedded IFRS within the legal structure governing finance in Europe.[4] Ever since, EU regulators have actively monitored and enforced IFRS standards, and a close feedback loop has been established between them and IASB. While the EU has not taken over IASB, it has firmly woven IFRS rules into the fabric of European markets. This, in turn, has hardened IASB-promoted soft law, not just in Europe but around the world. The formal commitment to IFRS has increased the incentive for EU policy-makers to promote the IFRS regime globally. Through regional embedding, IFRS have received the regulatory backing of EU regulators endowed with considerable delegated authority, including the ability to enforce rules extraterritorially. EU hardening has prompted the EU to more directly engage the IFRS governance process. As a result, the level of uncertainty surrounding the IFRS project has fallen considerably.

Since the EU imposed IFRS supranationally, it was not necessary for individual member states to adopt implementing legislation. Instead, national and European regulators are directly responsible for overseeing the implementation of IFRS standards for firms across all member states. Moreover, the EU created an endorsement process through which a technical committee vets IASB standards for use in Europe. In contrast to many loose harmonization processes where transnational regulatory co-operation gradually inspires domestic reform, the EU–IFRS process features a formal and robust mechanism for embedding transnational private actors within the regional rule-making process.

Since the EU adoption of IFRS in 2002, there has been tremendous movement toward standards diffusion. A host of countries including Brazil, Korea, Mexico, Canada, Australia, Japan, Russia and China either require IFRS standards or have largely integrated IFRS standards into national rules.[5] In many of these countries, IFRS is used as the standard not only for listed companies but all domestic firms. Most striking perhaps, the Securities and Exchange Commission (SEC) has decided to allow foreign issuers to use IFRS without reconciling to US Generally Accepted Accounting Principle (GAAP) and is currently considering permitting domestic issuers to do so as well (Posner 2010).

EU adoption brought IFRS to the tipping point, setting off a tidal wave of adoption around the world and instigating a convergence unimaginable just a few years earlier. This is more than a story about an epistemic community of experts or market convergence on a focal point. Rather, the key moment, not just regionally but globally, was the hardening of soft law through its formal embedding in EU regulation. As the Financial Reporting Council of Australia explained its decision to embrace IFRS:

> [the timing] is determined by the decision of the European Union to require EU listed companies to prepare their consolidated accounts in accordance with IASB standards from that date, in support of the EU single market objective. Australia certainly cannot afford to lag Europe in this regard. (Australian Financial Reporting Council 2002: 1)

A critical feature of the 2002 regulation was the inclusion of an equivalency clause that required the European Commission to evaluate national accounting standards in third countries and determine their relative compliance with IFRS (Posner 2010). In cases where the Commission deemed the jurisdiction's standards equivalent, firms could list in European markets without reconciliation. In order to determine equivalence, the European Securities and Markets Authority (ESMA) conducts an evaluation of a jurisdiction's standards and makes a recommendation to the Commission.[6] The ESMA has conducted reviews of a number of critical markets, such as Canada, South Korea and India. In the case of Canada and South Korea, ESMA deemed the standards equivalent. In the case of India, however, the ESMA has held out its ruling, waiting to determine the full extent of reforms and putting additional pressure on the Indian government to converge. As David Boymal, the former chairman of the Australian Accounting Standards Board, explained the motivation for Australian reform:

> This change [in Australia] has got a very strong political aspect because it was done without reference to the constituents and it was done as a matter of

> urgency and under immense pressure from the Europeans. (Durkin and Fenton-Jones 2008: 69)

EU equivalence tests, then, create a legal mechanism through which EU regulators can lend coercive pressure to their efforts of promoting IFRS globally.

EU regulators have used other tools as well to promote IFRS, including capacity-building, trainings, and direct lobbying at the national level. The legitimacy and financial resources of European regulators thus back up and strengthen the informal institution of the IASB. In the words of the European Commission:

> The Commission is in contact with authorities responsible for accounting from countries all around the world in order to cooperate in the creation of a single reporting framework for companies listed on international markets.
>
> In that respect, the EU is promoting convergence of accounting standards of third countries with the (IFRS). On the way to full convergence the EU proposed to accept certain third country national accounting standards as equivalent with IFRS (as adopted by the EU) in order to facilitate cross-border listings.[7]

The engagement by the EU with other jurisdictions has shored up certainty in IFRS. As the Financial Reporting Council of Australia explains:

> The meetings [facilitated by the EU] added significantly to our understanding of global trends in accounting and auditing standards, and audit independence matters. It was clear that there was a genuine commitment to convergence around the globe. (Australian Accounting Standards Board 2006: 17)

European integration has produced an intricate set of implementation and enforcement tools, which serve to give IFRS teeth and promote a common enforcement of IFRS within the EU and beyond. Starting in 2003, the European Commission tasked ESMA to create an enforcement network comprised of national supervisory authorities. This network, known as European Enforcers Coordination Sessions (EECS), serves as a co-ordination mechanism for implementation at the regional level. Each year it agrees on enforcement priorities, compiles enforcement actions in a collective database for the members, and publishes key cases.[8] As such, EECS is refining the enforcement process within Europe, honing its tasks, and embedding IFRS within regional administrative law. While this reduces the flexibility commonly associated with soft law rules, this hardening dramatically increases the certainty associated with their diffusion.

As part of endorsing IFRS standards, the EU has actively engaged IFRS governance. Much of the scholarly literature on IFRS rule-making has focused on specific instances of influence; for example, whether the EU has been able to shift the content of IFRS rules concerning financial instrument reporting known as IAS 39 (Botzem 2012; Leblond 2011). While widespread use of carve-outs and transposition adjustments might threaten the predictability of the regime, EU continued participation in the regime signals its overall commitment to the project (Mügge 2011). In particular, the EU has called for greater oversight of IASB by public sector actors to assure accountability. In the wake of the financial crisis, this became a major focus of the G20. IASB has amended its constitution to create a Monitoring Board, comprised of public sector officials including the European Commission. This Monitoring Board meets regulatory with the IASB and must approve the trustees that serve as the ultimate decision-makers in the organization. Supranational imposition of IFRS by the EU has catalyzed an important feedback loop in which public authorities are directly involved in IASB governance (Richardson and Eberlein 2011; Veron 2007). EU engagement of the IFRS process not only has the potential to shape IFRS standards, but also increases the incentive for other countries to join the standards governance process. As the Australian Financial Reporting Council explains, 'European countries are working more closely together to provide early and considered input to the global standard setting process, and this highlights the need for Australia and other countries in the Asian region to do likewise' (Australian Financial Reporting Council 2005).

The accounting standards case demonstrates the important interaction of regional law and international soft law. In particular, it dispels a purely technocratic or power-based account. The embedding of transnational standards regionally is transforming the character of the global regime both by increasing the incentive for the EU to promote the standard and by increasing the predictability of the standard for potential adopters.

DIFFUSION OF DERIVATIVES REGULATION THROUGH NATIONAL EMBEDDING

The case of close-out netting regulation for over-the-counter (OTC) derivatives illustrates the way that EU embedding of soft law rules has global consequences for diffusion, even when there is no direct supranational imposition. Rather than mandating a specific solution supranationally, as in the accounting case, EU directives merely required member states in general terms to provide for effective close-out netting. Subsequent domestic implementation debates provided the International Swaps and Derivatives Association (ISDA), a private body comprising more than 800 financial institutions, law firms and other industry stakeholders, with an ideal opportunity to shape domestic law according to its preferred soft law solution. While ISDA has actively promoted such standards around the world, EU member states offered a particularly fertile ground for transnational lobbying. The implementation of financial directives, such as the 1996 Investment Services Directive and the 2002 Directive on Financial Collateral Arrangements, unfroze the specific areas of law targeted by ISDA in initially 15 and eventually over two dozen markets near-simultaneously. Rapid adoption in the EU, in turn, generated momentum for the diffusion of close-out netting rules globally. This bottom–up case highlights a more subtle way in which the EU can boost confidence in a given set of soft law rules and thus catalyze their uptake.

OTC derivatives are private contracts between two or more entities that are negotiated directly between the parties and are generally not mediated by regulated stock exchanges. Trading in OTC derivatives has surged over the past two decades. The Bank of International Settlement estimates that between 1998 and 2010 outstanding notional amounts rose from $60 trillion to more than $600 trillion. By comparison, global gross domestic product (GDP) in 2011 stood at only $70 trillion.

In light of these mind-boggling amounts, regulators have long been concerned about their implication for systemic stability (Mügge 2009). The original Basel capital adequacy standards issued in 1988 required banks to hold reserves against the notional value, or face value, of their derivatives exposure to protect against possible counterparty default or insolvency (Matthews 1995). While notional exposure increases with each individual contract, systemic risk is linked to net exposure. To illustrate this, imagine two banks, Alter and Ego. Alter has a contract obligating it to pay Ego $100. Separately, Ego has agreed to pay Alter $50. The notional exposure of both is $150. Yet, if Alter goes bankrupt, Ego should only lose $50, for even though Alter can no longer pay it the promised $100, Ego also no longer has to pay Alter the separately promised $50. Once the claims are offset, the net exposure is $50. In 1994, after industry advocacy and expert support, the Basel Committee modified its standards, allowing domestic regulators to let financial institutions hold reserve capital in proportion to their net derivatives exposure (*Ibid.*).

To facilitate derivatives trading and reduce associated transactions costs, leading global financial institutions in 1985 founded ISDA. The stated mission of the association, which in 2013 had members from more than 60 countries, is 'to make over-the-counter (OTC) derivatives markets safe and efficient'.[9] To this end, ISDA created and maintains the ISDA Master Agreement, a lengthy derivatives contract that trading parties employ to avoid costly *ad hoc* contract drafting. Employing the Master Agreement makes all transactions between two parties legally part of the same contract and enables close-out netting. ISDA estimates that close-out netting has reduced the credit exposure of financial institutions by 85 per cent (Mengle 2010). Put differently, if it were not for close-out netting provisions, banks alone would have needed $500 billion in extra capital in 2010 (*Ibid.*).

Close-out netting only works if it is compatible with applicable bankruptcy laws. The exposure reduction offered by close-out netting provisions only applies when positions can be netted prior to any other aspects of wind-down, liquidation or bankruptcy. Otherwise, in the example cited above, Ego might be obligated to pay Alter the promised $50 and then try to recover its $100, or at least a fraction, in a drawn-out bankruptcy proceeding. Prudent regulation would require Ego to prepare for the worst case, thus holding reserves against the full $150.

While close-out netting was feasible in some countries, even in leading markets such as the US bankruptcy law was originally incompatible with it. To address this problem, ISDA and its allies embarked on an ambitious global lobby campaign (Riles 2008; Tsingou 2003). In 1996, the association adopted a 'Model Netting Act' and lobbied governments to adopt it. The text modified a country's bankruptcy and insolvency laws to explicitly allow for close-out netting in the case of counterparty default.

ISDA's efforts with respect to Slovenia illustrate the association's approach. In a letter dated 30 October 2009, just as the country prepared to implement Directive 2009/44/EC on Settlement Finality and Financial Collateral Arrangements, ISDA explained to the minister of justice, the minister of finance, and the Bank of Slovenia the concept of close-out netting and argued its alleged benefits:

> As a result of these uncertainties . . . financial institutions and institutional investors inside and outside Slovenia that deal with Slovenian counterparties in financial transactions are at a competitive disadvantage, because they cannot confidently net their derivatives exposures against their Slovenian counterparties or rely on the terms set forth in their contracts.[10]

The efforts paid off: within a year of ISDA's lobbying, Slovenia amended its bankruptcy and financial markets laws to provide legal certainty for close-out netting. This enabled ISDA to commission an affirmative expert legal opinion that its members have since relied on to justify holding reserves for trades with Slovenian counterparties against net exposure only.

Slovenia is merely a case in turn. All in all, at least 38 countries had modified their bankruptcy codes in line with ISDA proposals by 2011 (Biggins and Scott 2012; Morgen 2008). According to the association, 'The longstanding consensus among industry and policy makers suggests that close-out netting is one of the more successful examples of international legal and regulatory harmonization' (Mengle 2010: 2).

While ISDA and the transnational soft law network it represents deserve credit for advancing netting legislation, the EU played a pivotal role in the diffusion process. The EU's first foray into this area was in 1996, when it asked member states to allow their banking supervisors, 'when assessing the compulsory capital cover for credit risks from OTC derivatives, to take into account the risk reducing effect of types of bi-lateral netting agreements' (European Commission 1996). The Directive did not force member states to modify their bankruptcy laws to allow close-out netting. It merely created the legal basis for member states' banking supervisor to allow lower reserves *if* the country already allowed close-out netting. It thus generated demand for netting-enabled bankruptcy laws without addressing supply, thereby creating an opportunity structure for ISDA's private sector policy entrepreneurs. In an interview, a senior ISDA representative underscored the critical role EU directives play in providing the organization with a window to achieve legislative change across numerous member states.[11] At the time of the 1996 EU Directive, close-out netting was only possible in the United Kingdom (UK), the Netherlands, Ireland and Germany. In the three years following the Directive, a total of nine additional EU countries incorporated ISDA-promoted provisions modifying their bankruptcy laws.

Figure 1 compares graphically the rate of adoption of close-out netting rules for EU countries and non-EU countries. Spikes in EU member state adoption following the passage of each of the two critical directives in 1996 and 2002 are clearly noticeable. In contrast, non-EU countries do not show a similar spike in the second half of the 1990s and the spike in the following decade trails developments in the EU by several years. Moreover, the share of EU members among adopters, especially in the earlier period, is striking. In 1999, 11 of 17 countries permitting close-out netting were EU members. The EU share reached its peak in 2004, when 17 out of 25, or 68 per cent, of all adopters were EU members. Subsequently the share fell as adoption outside the EU accelerated, and by 2011 EU members constituted just 55 per cent of all jurisdictions that had adopted close-out netting provisions.

The observed diffusion pattern of close-out netting rules is broadly consistent with our expectations. While the EU did not supranationally impose a specific soft law standard, its 1996 and 2002 directives created demand at the member state level and opened up the domestic legislative process, an opportunity for targeted lobbying that ISDA seized. Both directives were followed by a sudden uptick in close-out netting adoption within the EU, in contrast to the more gradual trend elsewhere. Clearly the Basle Committee's original embrace of netting and ISDA's lobbying played key roles. But it was the EU's endorsement of the concept, combined with the opportunities directive implementation afforded ISDA across a whole set of member states, that built momentum for close-out netting. With critical mass, competitive dynamics kicked in. The more jurisdictions embrace close-out netting for domestic transactions, the greater the competitive disadvantage for those who do not.

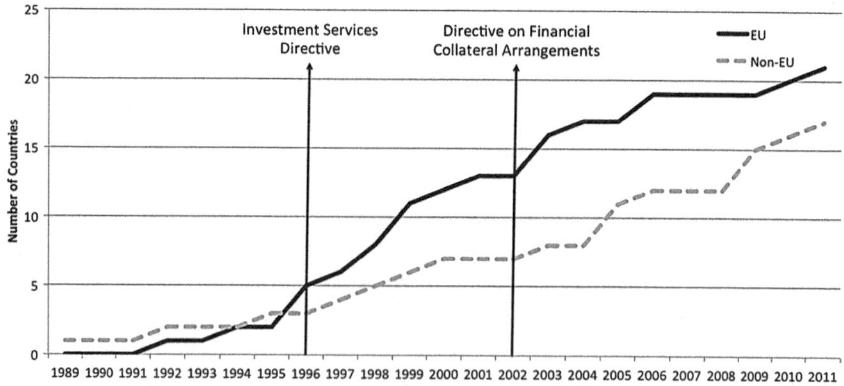

Figure 1 Modification of legislation to enable close-out netting, 1989–2011
Source: Authors' calculation using data from ISDA archive.

Moreover, the presence or absence of close-out netting provisions shapes capital flows. Given that leading US and British financial institutions can hold far less capital when trading derivatives with firms based in a jurisdiction were close-out netting is enabled than one where it is not, the former has a competitive advantage over the latter when it comes to attracting funds, regardless of the amount of domestic trading (Singer 2007).

The spread of close-out netting in the EU changed the calculus for other jurisdictions and provided important legitimacy for ISDA lobbying efforts. Critically, ISDA could leverage growing adoption across the EU as proof of concept, something it did directly and indirectly by enclosing an appendix of compliant jurisdictions with its outreach efforts.[12] While EU initiatives catalyzed adoption across member states, ISDA counted them as individual jurisdictions, thus creating a sense of important momentum. Within a year of the 1996 directive, when a review of Australian law suggested close-out netting might run into obstacles there, the head of the country's financial markets authority was alarmed: 'We are out of synch with the rest of the world. We need clarity, and the only way we can get clarity is to change the law' (Rogers 1997: 32). It is important to note that roughly two-thirds of this alleged 'rest of the world' were EU member states. Australia promptly modified its bankruptcy code to allow for close-out netting.

Similarly, the second wave of EU adoption triggered by the 2002 directive had repercussions elsewhere. In fact, the data show a slight lag after which diffusion among non-EU countries follows the pattern previously observed within the EU. Anecdotal empirical evidence suggests that advocates of pro-derivatives reform in many jurisdictions invoked 'international best practice', the role of ISDA and the EU, as well as the adverse competitive effects of remaining on the sidelines. Making the case for reform in the British Virgin Islands in 2007, financial lawyers Peter Tarn and Russell Willings argued:

> The combination of the EU's [2002] Financial Collateral Arrangements Directive and the adoption of netting legislation based on the ISDA Model Netting Act means that established practice in the derivatives market has been validated under corporate insolvency law in an increasing number of jurisdictions. (Tarn 2007: 32)

Importantly, even in 2013 rules across the EU were far from uniform. The 2002 directive went further than the original 1996 rules and explicitly asked member states to enable close-out netting.[13] Nevertheless, bankruptcy laws continue to vary across the EU and not all jurisdictions meet the threshold where close-out netting for all types of OTC derivatives is guaranteed. For these reasons, ISDA has lobbied the EU since 2008 for the adoption of a comprehensive netting directive to harmonize rules at the high end of netting provisions.[14] But even without supranational imposition, EU policy-making has been a potent catalyst of soft law hardening in Europe and global diffusion beyond.

In sharp contrast to the accounting case, however, the EU is far less engaged with ISDA than it is with IASB. EU officials neither actively endorse ISDA's private standards and benchmarks, nor have they sought to deliberately promote them through extraterritorial provisions or equivalency clauses. After EU member states supplied much of the critical mass, close-out netting rules have diffused through a combination of competitive pressure and ISDA lobbying. The diffusion process differs markedly from the case of accounting, where supranational imposition has given EU officials a much bigger transnational role. Nonetheless, the EU and the process of European financial integration were crucial for the spread of close-out netting regulation by catalyzing the hardening of ISDA standards through national embedding. This reduced the uncertainty surrounding the soft law rules, changed the calculus of follower jurisdictions, and boosted the legitimacy of ISDA claims as it lobbied non-European jurisdictions.

CONCLUSION

Ample research has shown that soft law is a staple of global finance and that the content of soft law rules and standards has distributional implications (Brummer 2011; Büthe and Mattli 2011; Oatley and Nabors 1998; Porter 2005a; Singer 2007). Earlier work has therefore focused on explaining the origins of various soft law networks (Kapstein 1992; Raustiala 2002; Zaring 1998), or has honed in on the influence and preference patterns shaping the content of rules and standards (Posner 2009a; Simmons 2001; Underhill and Zhang 2008; Mügge 2011). Our contribution broadens the debate by tracking how transnationally promulgated private standards interact with domestic law. We theorize that EU integration plays a key role in hardening soft law standards and find empirical support for two distinct causal pathways: supranational imposition and national embedding. We hypothesize that EU hardening shapes subsequent diffusion dynamics of soft law standards, and preliminary evidence is consistent with our expectations. EU hardening changes the calculus of follower jurisdictions, which in turn promotes adoption. This is especially the case for soft law incorporated in the EU via supranational imposition, because it gives EU officials a direct stake in the global soft law standards and enables the use of EU-level extraterritorial levers, such as the equivalency clause in accounting, in support of hastening global diffusion. But even in cases of national embedding, we find evidence that early and rapid adoption of a soft law standard in a large number of EU member states promotes adoption elsewhere. Our research, therefore, suggests that future studies of soft law diffusion, particular in global finance, should take EU membership, and the effects of domestic and regional law, into account.

More generally, our findings add an important caveat to skepticism regarding the role of soft law in global finance. Some critics have dismissed soft law networks because of their 'thin' level of institutionalization. The dynamics we have uncovered suggest that domestic rule-making forms part of the broader institutional fabric surrounding global soft law, and that domestic structures can give soft law a much 'thicker' degree of institutionalization than initially meets the eye (Helleiner and Pagliari 2011; Shaffer and Pollack 2009). The contribution adds to a growing literature that explores how private international law increasingly mixes with domestic regulation (Kaczmarek and Newman 2011; Lavelle 2011; Putnam 2009).

The evidence we have presented goes beyond standard rationalist accounts' focus on market and reputational incentives as the principal drivers of soft law adoption (e.g., Simmons 2001) and calls into question skeptics' view of soft law as epiphenomenal to great power interests and toothless owing to the underlying institutions lacking monitoring and enforcement capabilities (Abbott and Snidal 2000; Drezner 2007; Kahler and Lake 2009). However, not all of this is good news for soft law proponents. The speed and flexibility of such soft law standards has been held up in the literature as this form of governance's principal strength (Raustiala 2002; Slaughter 2004; Vabulas and Snidal 2013). Yet some of this speed and flexibility is lost as soft law becomes hardened. In fact, domestic hardening has a similar effect on private international law as does domestic treaty ratification in the case of public international law. Henceforth, transnational standard-setters cannot advance too far ahead of lead adopters such as the EU and may have to give public officials from lead adopters a formal voice in the process.

The Janus-faced nature of hardening for proponents of soft law – increasing its predictability, which spurs adoption while reducing its flexibility – raises the stakes for those interested in the normative implications of the standards involved. Rules like IFRS and close-out netting provisions have significant market consequences with potent distributional implications. Whether supranational imposition in Europe, and its effects on global diffusion of IFRS or netting rules, is a good thing depends on a given stakeholder's vantage point and the comparison to the respective *status quo ante*. Arguably, the harmonization of accounting standards has reduced transactions costs for cross-listing, boosted liquidity and thereby reduced the cost of financing. But not everybody will agree this is a good thing or that IFRS was the only way to achieve this. With close-out netting rules, the picture is even murkier. Such rules are clearly beneficial if the goal is to promote derivatives trading. However, in light of the role complex derivatives played in the financial crisis that began with the meltdown in US subprime mortgage-backed securities markets, critics might well argue that promoting derivatives trading is the last thing governments should do. While we do not take a position on these legitimate questions, we would argue that understanding how EU financial integration promotes the global spread of soft law, and how hardening makes these standards more sticky, is of interest to both proponents and opponents of a given soft law standard in global finance.

The most obvious area for future research raised by our study concerns how EU hardening interacts with other components of diffusion processes (Simmons and Elkins 2004). Transposition can vary and there is a growing literature attempting to explore the determinants of such variation (Botzem 2012; Eberlein and Richardson 2012; Sharman 2011). Future work should not only scrutinize how competition and mimesis affect adoption within the EU in cases of national embedding, but also how these factors come together in influencing non-EU jurisdictions. Moreover, future research should explore how the two distinct causal pathways for hardening might shape diffusion patters after adoption such as interdependent implementation and enforcement (Bach and Newman 2010).

Equally important is to explore how well the notion of soft law hardening travels beyond Europe and our two cases. We have argued that the ongoing process of EU financial market re-regulation provides ample opportunities for supranational imposition and national embedding, making the EU a prime hardening agent. While the motivation for transnational standards adoption is outside the scope of this contribution, this last point presents an important boundary condition for the argument. We would expect hardening to be more likely during periods of extensive market-making and re-regulation. Moreover, the case studies highlight the importance of internal policy paralysis as a precondition for the adoption of transnational rules. It was, for example, the clash of systems driven by different models of national accounting standards within the member states that made IFRS an attractive alternative to the Commission as opposed to home grown solutions. None of this means, however, that hardening is an exclusive EU domain. Complimentary studies examining the interaction of transnational soft law and domestic regulation in the US seem consistent with our findings (Lavelle 2011). Similarly, the pattern that we identify in accounting and derivatives appears in other sectors, such as banking and auditing, where the EU has embedded transnational soft law into regional legislation.[15]

Our study suggests that soft law in global finance may not be so soft after all. The EU in particular plays a crucial role in hardening soft law through regional embedding, which in turn promotes the formal adoption of soft law standards in other jurisdictions. While EU hardening significantly reduces the risk of standards fragmentation, it also, paradoxically, makes the standard less flexible and amendable to change. Our findings are not the last word on this topic and we have identified several open questions as areas for future research. What they suggest even at this point, however, is that the pieces comprising the tapestry of global governance – transnational private governance, European integration and domestic law – in finance are increasingly intertwined.

Biographical notes: Abraham L. Newman is an associate professor at the BMW Center for German and European Studies in the Edmund A. Walsh School of Foreign Service at Georgetown University. David Bach is Senior Associate Dean and Senior Lecturer for Global Business and Politics at Yale School of Management.

ACKNOWLEDGMENTS

We would like to thank the editors, as well as two anonymous reviewers, who made invaluable suggestions. In addition, we thank participants at the conference on Europe and Global Finance organized by Daniel Mügge at the University of Amsterdam, 14–15 February 2013. In addition, we received very useful feedback from Burkard Eberlein, Calvin Huntington, Rahul Kaul, Stefano Pagliari, Tony Porter, Elliot Posner, Lucia Quaglia, Eleni Tsingou, Kevin Young, David Zaring and Jonathan Zeitlin.

NOTES

1 In terms of institutionalization, we follow Ruggie (1998: 2) who focuses on predictability of behavior structured in large part by organizational routines. He identifies international organizations with their bureaucratic capacities as the key mechanism for institutionalization internationally. Given the non-treaty-based nature of soft law, many observers have described them as thinly institutionalized or network-based. See, for example, Zaring (2004).

2 'The provisions in ... Directive 2006/49/EC of the European Parliament and of the Council of 14 June 2006 on the capital adequacy of investment firms and credit institutions (4), form an equivalent to the provisions of the Basel framework agreement.' Directive 2006/48/EC of the European Parliament and the Council of 14th June 2006 relating to the taking up and pursuit of the business of credit institutions. *Official Journal of the European Union*, 30 July 2006: L 177.

3 We refer to the organization as the IASB. Prior to 1999, the organization was named the International Accounting Standards Committee (IASC).

4 Regulation (EC) No 1606/2002 of the European Parliament and of the Council of 19 July 2002 on the application of international accounting standards. *Official Journal of the European Communities*, 11 September 2002: L 243.

5 http://www.iasplus.com/en/resources/ifrs-topics/use-of-ifrs (accessed 12 February 2014).

6 Prior to the financial crisis, ESMA was known as the Committee of European Securities Regulators (CESR).

7 http://ec.europa.eu/internal_market/accounting/third_countries/index_en.htm

8 See http://www.esma.europa.eu/page/IFRS-Enforcement-0 (accessed 12 February 2014).

9 'About ISDA', available at http://www2.isda.org/about-isda/ (accessed 26 January 2013)

10 Letter dated 30 October 2009 by Peter M. Werner of ISDA to Aleš Zalar, Minister of Justice of Slovenia, available at http://www.isda.org/speeches/pdf/SVN_NettingLtr-MoJ_v1.pdf (accessed 9 February 2013).

11 Interview with ISDA official.

12 See ISDA comment letters to jurisdictions at http://www.isda.org/speeches/comments.html (accessed 9 February 2013).

13 See Article 7 of Directive 2002/47/EC of the European Parliament and of the Council of 6 June 2002 on financial collateral arrangements.

14 'ISDA proposes harmonization of netting in Europe', Press Release, 17 April 2008.

15 The 2006 EU Capital Adequacy Directive and the 2006 Auditing Directive both rely on international standards. The Auditing Directive is still awaiting implementation.

REFERENCES

Abbott, K. and Snidal, D. (2000) 'Hard and soft law in international governance', *International Organization* 54(3): 421–56.

Alexander, K., Dhumale, R. and Eatwell, J. (2006) *Global Governance of Financial Systems: The International Regulation of Systemic Risk*, Oxford: Oxford University Press.

Australian Accounting Standards Board (2006) *Annual Report 2005–2006*, Canberra: Australian Accounting Standards Board.

Australian Financial Reporting Council (2002) 'Adoption of international accounting standards', *Bulletin of the Financial Reporting Council* 4, 3 July: 1–3.

Australian Financial Reporting Council (2005) *Annual Report 2004–2005*, available at http://www.frc.gov.au/reports/2004_2005/03_FRC.asp (accessed February 2014).

Bach, D. (2010) 'Varieties of cooperation: the domestic institutional roots of global governance', *Review of International Studies* 36(3): 561–89.

Bach, D. and Newman, A.L. (2007) 'The European regulatory state and global public policy: micro-institutions and macro-influence', *Journal of European Public Policy* 16(4): 827–46.

Bach, D. and Newman, A.L. (2010) 'Transgovernmental networks and domestic policy convergence: evidence from insider trading regulation', *International Organization* 64(3): 505–28.

Barr, M. and Miller, G. (2006) 'Global administrative law: the view from Basel', *European Journal of International Law* 17(1): 15–46.

Biggins, J. and Scott, C. (2012) 'Public – private relations in a transnational private regulatory regime: ISDA, the state and OTC derivatives market reform', *European Business Organization Law Review* 13: 309–46.

Borzel, T. and Risse, T. (2000) 'When Europe hits home: Europeanization and domestic change', *European Integration online Papers* 4(15), available at http://eiop.or.at/eiop/texte/2000-015a.htm (accessed 12 February 2014).

Botzem, S. (2012) *Politics of Accounting Regulation*, Cheltenham: Edward Elgar Publishing.

Botzem, S. and Quack, S. (2009) '(No) limits to Anglo-American accounting? Reconstructing the history of the International Accounting Standards Committee: a review article', *Accounting, Organizations and Society* 34(8): 988–98.

Brummer, C. (2011) *Soft Law and the Global Financial System: Rule Making in the 21st Century*, Cambridge: Cambridge University Press.

Büthe, T. and Mattli, W. (2011) *The New Global Rulers: The Privatization of Regulation in the World Economy*, Princeton, NJ: Princeton University Press.

Caporaso, J. and Tarrow, S. (2009) 'Polanyi in Brussels: supranational institutions and the transnational embedding of markets', *International Organization* 63(4): 593–620.

Davies, H. and Green, D. (2008) *Global Financial Regulation: The Essential Guide*, Cambridge: Polity Press.

Drezner, D. (2007) *All Politics is Global: Explaining International Regulatory Regimes*, Princeton, NJ: Princeton University Press.

Dunoff, J.L. and Pollack, M.A. (eds) (2012) *Interdisciplinary Perspectives on International Law and International Relations: The State of the Art*, Cambridge: Cambridge University Press.

Durkin, P. and Fenton-Jones, M. (2008) 'Call to account on standards', *Australian Financial Review*, 26 November, p. 69.

Eaton, S.B. (2005) 'Crisis and the consolidation of international accounting standards: Enron, the IASB, and America', *Business and Politics* 7(3): 22–40.

Eberlein, B. and Newman, A.L. (2008) 'Escaping the international governance dilemma? Incorporated transgovernmental networks in the European Union', *Governance* 21(1): 25–52.

Eberlein, B. and Richardson, A. (2012) 'Accounting for implementation: international standards in accounting', Unpublished manuscript.
European Commission (1996) 'Derivatives: contractual netting directive adopted,' IP/96/172, 26 February.
Farrell, H. (2003) 'Constructing the international foundations of e-commerce: the EU-US safe harbor arrangement', *International Organization* 57: 277–306.
Featherstone, K. and Radaelli, C. (2003) *The Politics of Europeanization*, Oxford: Oxford University Press.
Goldstein, J., Kahler, M., Keohane, R.O. and Slaughter, A.-M. (2000) 'Introduction: legalization and world politics', *International Organization* 54(3): 385–99.
Helleiner, E. and Pagliari, S. (2011) 'The end of an era in international financial regulation', *International Organization* 65(1): 169–200.
Hooghe, L. and Marks, G. (2003) 'Unraveling the central state, but how? Types of multi-level governance', *American Political Science Review* 97(2): 233–43.
Joachim, J. (2003) 'Framing issues and seizing opportunities: the UN, NGOs, and women's rights', *International Studies Quarterly* 47(2): 247–74.
Kaczmarek, S. and Newman, A.L. (2011) 'The long arm of the law: extraterritoriality and the national implementation of foreign bribery legislation', *International Organization* 65(4): 745–70.
Kahler, M. and Lake, D. (2009) 'Economic integration and global governance: why so little supranationalism?', in W. Mattli and N. Woods, (eds), *The Politics of Global Regulation*, Princeton, NJ: Princeton University Press, pp. 242–76.
Kapstein, E. (1992) 'Between power and purpose: central bankers and the politics of regulatory convergence', *International Organization* 46(1): 265–87.
Lavelle, K. (2011) 'Bringing the government back in: implementing the Basle agreements in American governing institutions.' Unpublished manuscript.
Leblond, P. (2011) 'EU, US and international accounting standards: a delicate balancing act in governing global finance', *Journal of European Public Policy* 18(3): 443–61.
Matthews, B.C. (1995) 'Capital adequacy, netting, and derivatives', *Stanford Journal of Law, Business and Finance* 2(1): 167–91.
Mattli, W. and Büthe, T. (2005) 'Accountablity in accounting? The politics of private rule-making in the public interest', *Governance* 18(3): 399–430.
Mengle, D. (2010) 'The importance of close-out netting', *ISDA Research Notes*, 1 November.
Morgan, G. (2008) 'Market formation and governance in international financial markets: the case of OTC derivatives', *Human Relations* 51(5): 637–60.
Mügge, D. (2009) 'Tales of tails and dogs: derivatives and financialization in contemporary capitalism', *Review of International Political Economy* 16(3): 514–26.
Mügge, D. (2011) 'The European presence in global financial governance: a principal–agent perspective', *Journal of European Public Policy* 18(3): 383–402.
Newman, A.L. (2008) *Protectors of Privacy: Regulating Personal Data in the Global Economy*, Ithaca, NY: Cornell University Press.
Nölke, A. and Perry, J. (2007) 'The power of transnational private governance: financialization and the IASB', *Business and Politics* 9(3): 1–27.
Oatley, T. and Nabors, R. (1998) 'Redistributive cooperation: market failure, wealth transfers, and the Basle Accord', *International Organization* 52(1): 35–54.
Perry, J. and Nölke, A. (2005) 'International accounting standard setting: a network approach', *Business and Politics* 7(3), doi: 10.2202/1469-3569.1136.
Perry, J. and Nölke, A. (2006) 'The political economy of international accounting standards', *Review of International Political Economy* 13(4): 559–86.
Porter, T. (2005a) *Globalization and Finance*. Cambridge: Polity Press.
Porter, T. (2005b) 'Private authority, technical authority, and the globalization of accounting standards', *Business and Politics* 7(3), doi: 10.2202/1469-3569.1138.

Posner, E. (2009a) 'Making rules for global finance: transatlantic regulatory cooperation at the turn of the millennium', *International Organization* 63(4): 665–99.
Posner, E. (2009b) *The Origins of Europe's New Stock Markets*, Cambridge, MA: Harvard University Press.
Posner, E. (2010) 'Sequence as explanation: the international politics of accounting standards', *Review of International Political Economy* 17(4): 639–64.
Powell, E. and Staton, J. (2009) 'Domestic judicial institutions and human rights treaty violations', *International Studies Quarterly* 53(1): 149–74.
Putnam, T.L. (2009) 'Courts without borders: domestic sources of US extraterritoriality in the regulatory sphere', *International Organization* 63(3): 459–90.
Quaglia, L. (2010) *Governing Financial Services in the European Union: Banking,Securities and Post-Trading*, London: Routledge.
Quaglia, L. (2014) 'The sources of European Union influence in international financial regulatory fora', *Journal of European Public Policy* 21(3), doi: 10.1080/13501763.2014.882970.
Raustiala, K. (2002) 'The architecture of international cooperation: transgovernmental networks and the future of international law', *Virginia Journal of International Law* 43: 1–93.
Richardson, A.J. and Eberlein, B. (2011) 'Legitimating transnational standard setting: the case of the International Accounting Standards Board', *Journal of Business Ethics* 98 (2) 217–45.
Riles, A. (2008) 'The anti-network: private global governance, legal knowledge, and the legitimacy of the state', *American Journal of Comparative Law* 56(3): 605–30.
Rogers, I. (1997) 'Lobby seeks action on netting law', *Australian Financial Review*, 7 July, p. 32.
Ruggie, J. (1998) *Constructing the World Polity*, London: Routledge.
Sabel, C. and Zeitlin, J. (2010) *Experimentalist Governance in the European Union: Towards a New Architecture*, Oxford: Oxford University Press.
Shaffer, G.C. and Pollack, M.A. (2009) 'Hard vs soft law: alternatives, complements, and antagonists in international governance', *Minnesota Law Review* 94: 706–99.
Sharman, J.C. (2011) 'Testing the global financial transparency regime', *International Studies Quarterly* 55(4): 981–1001.
Simmons, B. (2001) 'The international politics of harmonization: the case of capital market regulation', *International Organization* 55(3): 589–620.
Simmons, B. and Elkins, Z. (2004) 'The globalization of liberalization: policy diffusion in the international political economy', *American Political Science Review* 98(1): 171–89.
Singer, D.A. (2007) *Regulating Capital: Setting Standards for the International Financial System*, Ithaca, NY: Cornell University Press.
Slaughter, A.-M. (2004) *A New World Order*, Princeton, NJ: Princeton University Press.
Tarn, P. and Willings, R. (2007), 'The BVI is regarded as one of the world's leading offshore jurisdictions, with derivatives being a particular strength,' *The Lawyer*, 25 June.
Tarullo, D.K. (2008) *Banking on Basel: The Future of International Financial Regulation*, Washington, DC: Peterson Institute.
Tsingou, E. (2003) 'Transnational policy communities and financial governance: the role of private actors in derivatives regulation', Working Paper, Coventry: University of Warwick.
Underhill, G.R.D. and Zhang, X. (2008) 'Setting the rules: private power, political underpinnings, and legitimacy in global monetary and financial governance', *International Affairs* 84(3): 535–54.
Vabulas, F. and Snidal, D. (2013) 'Organization without delegation', *Review of International Organization* 8(2): 193–220.

Veron, N. (2007) *The Global Accounting Experiment*, Brussels: Bruegel.
Weir, M and Skocpol, T. (1985) 'State structures and the possibilities for Keynesian responses to the Great Depression', in P. Evans, D. Rueschemeyer and T. Skocpol (eds), *Bringing the State Back in*, Cambridge: Cambridge University Press, pp. 107–68.
Zaring, D. (1998) 'International law by other means: the twilight existence of international financial regulatory organizations', *Texas International Law Journal* 33: 281–330.
Zaring, D. (2004) 'Informal procedure, hard and soft, in international administration', *Chicago Journal of International Law* 5: 547–604.

Index

Note: Page numbers in **bold** type refer to figures
Page numbers in *italic* type refer to tables
Page numbers followed by 'n' refer to notes

For Product Safety Concerns and Information please contact our EU representative GPSR@taylorandfrancis.com Taylor & Francis Verlag GmbH, Kaufingerstraße 24, 80331 München, Germany

Batch number: 10725973

Printed by Printforce, the Netherlands